TOWER OF LIGHT

TOWER OF LIGHT
Artist's near death experience to help YOU never give UP

Misa Art

Copyright © MISA ART
All rights reserved. No part of this publication may be reproduced , distributed, or transmitted in any form or by any means, including photocopying, recording or other electronic or mechanical methods, with the prior written permission of the publisher, except in the case of brief quotations embodied in critical reviews and certain other noncommercial uses permitted by copyright law.
For Permission requests, write to innovator Misa ART, misa@gmail.com or
 www.misa-artwork.com,(contact). Addressed " ATTENTION: Permissions Coordinator"

This book is based on life events of Misa Art and her experiences during her near-death experience. However, this book is not intended to give medical information or advice, and the reader is encouraged to consult an appropriate professional on all health, mental health issues.
The information contained in this book is unintended to be inspirational and not for diagnosis, prescription, or treatment of any health or psychological disorder whatsoever. Neither Author nor people in this book have engaged in rendering professional advice or services to this book are not intended to substitute for consulting with your physician, psychologist or other healthcare provider on all matters of concern, including suicidal thoughts. All matters regarding you health require medical supervision chosen by you.
Neither the author or people in this story shall be liable for any loss or damage allegedly arisen from the information or suggestion in this book. The information should not replace consolation with competent healthcare of mental health professional. The author and people in this book are in no way liable for any misuse of the material contained in this book.

Special Thank you to those who worked with me on this book:
Cover design, book design: Greg Gorski, cybertoast.com
Cover architectural design of Tower of Light project:
Douglas Hammen, douglasdesign.us
Cover painting of "Religiosa" by Misa Art, misa-artwork.com
Edit: Livia Romano
Support Edit: Karen Hastings, karenhastings.wordpress.com
Photography of Misa Art: Sarka Holeckova, sarkaphotography.com
Jana Behenska, czech friend, co-worker on some mottos, translated this book into czech version
Jordan Fletcher, friend co-writer Deepak Chopra, wrote last motto of each 12 chapters
Helena Breese

Magical Thank you to those who are featured in this book:
Dr. Tom Voitas, chiropractor, shaman
Kath Carter, dear king, musiccityhitmakers.com, #MHMC
Bogdan Bosak and family, chicagometalsupply.com
Douglas Hammen, my main architect, douglasdesign.us
Gina Fontanini, dear friend, filmaker, la-gproductions.com
Karen and John...Thiel, supporter, friend, karenthiel.cabionline.com
Zenon Kurdziel, ridgelandassociates.com
Mary Carol Fitzgerald, photographer friend, marycarolfitzgerald.com
Juan de dios Kucho, Peruvian shaman
Lukas Szwalec, video maker, Reena Prema Spacefacebeauty.com, Sue and Leonard Socinski

Thank you to all who pledge for me in Kickstarter to
make this book happen!!
YOU ARE ALL AMAZING.

Dedicated to my grandmother Emilie, my beautiful angel in heaven.

Thank you from bottom of my heart to my shaman Dr. Tom Voitas and my dear 'KING' Kath Carter

Gratitude to all of my friends in this book and those who are not in it.

Acceptance for those who gave me a lesson from the past and who will in the future.

Love to my family, to my soul family too.

Grace to all of my Ancestors and Angels.

I AM in the LIGHT AND LOVE.

Contents

1. Ghost Party on My Body 12
2. Dreams of Predictions 34
3. Sweat and Fear 46
4. Flying Geisha 58
5. Angels, Prayers 78
6. The Power of Manifestation 88
7. Native American Indians 98
8. King and Priest 116
9. Amma 128
10. Tarot Reader: Eagles and Pigeons 138
11. Soulmates and Twin-Flames 150
12. Mamacocha 160
13. Tower of Light 182

Preface

"I should write a book? Nonsense! I am a visual artist, not a writer," I said and smiled at her.

She smiled back. Her hands were crossed, the same as her legs. She was drawing an imaginary "X" symbol with her body. Suddenly, a stream of light hit a little pile of magic cards in front of her. With no words, she answered. Sometimes to understand, we have to listen first. Sometimes there are no words. Sometimes the information comes in very unusual ways. Very unexpected.

Well, that is how it happened to me. This is a true story.

I would like to thank all of YOU who, during these years, believed in me and those who will start to believe in something beautiful after reading this book. To write this story meant to be vulnerable. I hope to encourage you to be brave and share your own story too, whichever way you find comfortable. I don't think that we can always see or understand the full impact that we can have on each other. Maybe the full realization comes only when we finally see the light.

My talent and spiritual gifts that I received were given to me only to give back – to build the Tower of Light for YOU.

Chapter 1

Ghost party on my Body

Tower of Light

Ghost Party on My Body

I was standing in front of his door. I was a bit scared, but I knew that I needed help. I needed help with everything—and at that point, I would have taken it from anyone. Up until then my usual habit in reaching out to others for support was simply never to do it. I didn't know *how* to do it—but there I was, sitting in his lobby and staring at his door. My mind was racing; it was full of memories.

The previous week, I had spent a night experiencing unusual visions and sounds. I shared the story with a friend from yoga. I had seen spirits and colors around people, and I was freaked out—who wouldn't be? As I explained the weird experience, my friend smiled and said, "Here, take this number."

"Who is he, a doctor for nutcases? A witch doctor?" I laughed, trying to make a joke. I always joke when I am nervous or if I feel like I am losing my mind. As an artist, that feeling seems to happen often—maybe even all the time. *Am I losing my mind?*

"No, silly, he is a chiropractor—but a special one. He is a shaman as well." My friend gave me a hug.

I needed that hug. In that moment, I got a warm feeling that everything would be OK, and felt love for my friend and all those people who show up in your life just to give you a hug or smile.

"Please come in," he said. His warm, calm voice emanated from behind the door and broke the stream of memories rising in my mind. I got up and slowly moved to the door. My heart started racing. *Now I will see this crazy shaman*, my mind said. *Oh well, aren't we all weirdos anyway?* a second voice said. *I need help. I need help. I can do this...*, a third voice echoed inside.

He was nothing like how I imagined a shaman would be. He was standing there in the middle of a dark room, quiet. I couldn't tell his age—maybe 50? I noticed his grey, funky hair. *Shamans wear jeans? Well, it's kind of a modern approach, I guess.* I smiled nervously and walked in. It was a bit cold, but his blue eyes were warm. The little voice in my head said *breathe Misa, breathe*, like you might tell yourself before skydiving out of an airplane.

"Hi, I'm Misa and I am here because…" I started to talk out loud, like I always do when I am nervous. His voice stopped me. "I know," he said. I felt love and kindness coming from his heart. His body wasn't large, but his spiritual-heart was huge—I could see it; I could feel it—it was palpable. I looked at him very closely and realized that he can freaking *see* things! *He sees everything. He is a seer. He is peering into my soul.* I suddenly felt so NAKED! *Oh my God, he sees you, he sees you. He sees your spirit, your past, your father... Wow. Oh, my father...* I started to feel a rush of anger. *He sees how he abused you... He sees how crazy you are. He sees all your fears. He sees all, good and bad—wait, he sees your ghosts, too!* In that moment, I panicked and wanted to run far away.

But I didn't—something kept me there. Maybe it was him, maybe it was me; maybe it was spirit working through both of us.

Tower of Light

"Please stand by a window," he said as he smiled again. I moved slowly into the light, and my big blue eyes widened; my blond hair started to shine in the ray of light that was beaming into this dark room full of strange little statues. They seemed to be from many places in this world: a true shaman's collection.

"You had a strong connection with your grandmother," he continued. Instantly I wanted to cry. My heart got heavy. *I miss her. How I miss her.* More than anyone else, she was my life guru. She had passed away four years before. In fact, that's when all of this madness really started—visions, sounds, and dreams; the things I knew about people as soon they entered my art studio, as soon they looked at me; the sudden certainty something more than simple circumstance was influencing the way events unfolded in my life. I knew there was more to life than the physical world: there was an invisible realm of spirit that only people like this shaman and other seers could perceive.

"Yes," I whispered. "Do you see her?" I asked quickly, my voice was filled with hope.

"No," he replied, "I feel her." He smiled again. *Smiling a bit much,* I thought, *for a shaman—aren't they supposed to be serious?* He was very quietly staring somewhere next to me, close to my legs. Not in a sexual way, but as if he was looking into invisible realms. It was a very vulnerable and uncomfortable feeling for me. I felt like a crazy person. *He is a shaman,* I thought, *I guess he knows what he's doing… but then again, this is starting to be weird.* Then he looked at me and smiled again. I could see in his bright blue eyes that he was reading my thoughts.

Misa Art

Oh, shit… Stop, mind, stop talking! Hello brain, stop! He can hear you! You are safe, you are safe.

"You are safe," he said. *Yep, he can read my mind.* "Please, lie down on the massage table right here." He pointed to a high table with Native American blankets on it.

*This is going to be a massage session now? I am not sure if I should lie down and let this man touch me, because who knows what is going to happen. I don't trust men. Why can't there be any shaman women her*e? I pretended that I was fine and had no fear. Quickly I jumped on the top of the table and sat up straight. *OK,* I thought, *ready for some chiropractor time, or reiki?* I had no idea what he was going to do, but I hoped he knew what he was doing.

"Just relax and lie down," he said as he slowly moved over to where I lay on the table. He sat down on a bench by my feet with a colorful little drum in his hands. *Well, this doesn't seem like a yoga lesson or massage so far. Music time, maybe?* My mind wandered to different possibilities. I noticed that he had lots of weird-looking shaman-doctor gadgets. I was starting to feel that this whole "shaman" experience was, maybe, a bit too funky for me.

In a modern high-rise tower in Chicago, in the middle of a city with millions of people, here I was with this urban-looking shaman. *Only me,* I thought… *crazy people find crazy people.* You attract what you are, or whatever you think you are.

Tower of Light

I finally lay down and stretched my colorful, long dress out as far as it could go. I remembered that I had no shoes on—he had told me to take them off a couple of minutes before. *Now he is sitting by my feet.* I hoped they weren't dirty. *Kinda like when you show up for yoga practice with dirty feet—ugh, I hate those moments. No, they are clean, they are clean, luckily I remembered.*

His music stopped my thoughts. He started to sing while tapping on his drum. He closed his eyes. I blinked at my feet. He looked like he was enjoying the whole process. I still had no idea what was going on. What was I supposed to do? He hadn't given me any instructions, and there was no "WHAT TO DO WHEN YOU MEET A SHAMAN" sign up on the walls. *Hmmm... I guess I'll close my eyes.* I felt tired suddenly. *How much will all this cost me? Is there a fee for him giving me this psychic reading or whatever it is? Do all shamans work by the hour? Does he work nine to five or what?* As an artist, I hadn't sold anything for the past couple of weeks. That's the thing with artists—always a lack of money.

The shaman started to sing in Spanish. I could only smile. At the time, I was learning Spanish along with four other languages. I could understand only a couple of words between the beats of his drum. He sang something like, "My sister here needs help, and healing..." He continued. *Mi hermanita? This Polish-looking dude is full of surprises. Me? A sister?* I smiled. I finally relaxed my body, and the sound started to match the rhythm of my heartbeat. Faster and louder—it kept getting louder! With closed eyes I started to feel cold—a cold sensation from behind my eyelids. I saw something above me move. *Oh no!* I felt chills cover my entire body and a feeling of a tight throat. *What a strange experience!*

Misa Art

You are not alone, Misa. The shaman is here. It is the middle of the day. This is not a nightmare. You are not sleeping. The voice inside my head was talking. *Wait! I am not sleeping, I am awake!* That sudden insight made me feel worse. There was movement—I could feel energy. It got faster. The movement reminded me of when you don't know how to slow down the speed of a ceiling fan. *Oh no, I should open my eyes. No wait, don't open my eyes… I don't want to feel or see THEM—the spirits. Oh no, THEY ARE HERE! I AM GOING TO DIE!*

I opened my eyes in panic. I saw a cloud of dark smoke spinning into a circle above me to the rhythm of the drum. I recognized the spirits. I had seen THEM before, but not like this—not like a huge parade of smoke. This whirlpool of dark energy above me started to get bigger and bigger, and move faster and faster. *I AM GOING TO DIE! Right here on this table!* I started to feel the black stone on my chest, which he had put on me earlier. It was getting heavier. I started to breathe faster. I felt tears coming from my eyes, down the sides of my cheeks. The smoke started to take the shape of an object—but I couldn't see what it was. There was a feeling of hands. *THEY are creating a hand to touch me.* A long, smoky hand from the circle on the ceiling extended toward me!

It was coming closer and closer. I closed my eyes in fear and felt the pressure of the stone on my heart. The dark spirit hand was pushing and pushing. I couldn't hear my heart anymore, and the pressure in my ears was making an annoying ringing sound. I was frozen. *So, this is how people die?* I thought. At that moment, I once again became aware of the music, and another voice started to sing while this strange shaman—funky, yet deep—was still working by my feet. *I know this beautiful voice; I know it!* Tears were hot, running down my cheeks. *Grandma! My Grandma's voice!* She was singing with him.

Tower of Light

I suddenly had a feeling like all these beings—living and dead, known and unknown—were gathered as if for a party in my honor, right there on the massage table. And attending this ghost party table was not only my body, but also my deepest fears. Something gently touched my hand. I knew it wasn't human. No one was standing there.

The dark stone got lighter on my chest. I exhaled. I didn't realize that I had been holding my breath all that time. *You are safe.* This voice came from my heart, it was not coming from my mind— and I knew for sure that the voice wasn't mine. *You are safe,* it said again. There was still a peaceful crystal that the shaman had placed in the middle of my forehead and it had, by this time, gotten cold. *Yes, he did put it there before I lay down.*

A feeling of peace started washing over me. The smoke disappeared, and I had a vision of a young, handsome warrior on a horse. He moved his sword and *chop, chop!* He chopped heads off. I kept feeling shocked and outraged that he was chopping the heads off people—but then I realized that the warrior was me. *It can't be—stop, stop!*

I shook my body. The visions disappeared. The music stopped.

I looked down toward my feet. He was still sitting there, holding his drum—*this guy who calls himself a shaman*, I thought. My mind was still trying to make sense of everything that had just happened. *What the hell was that?* I sat up, all confused. I looked at him and couldn't even speak. *Hello, hello, I almost died here! Did you see that?* I wanted to yell at him. I could feel my anger.

"This time you didn't see too much, maybe next session," he said calmly.

"Whaaat?" I replied. *Is he serious?*

"Just kidding," he started to laugh. Right there, I knew we were going to be good friends.

"You should try a sweat lodge," he continued.

I don't know what a sweat lodge is, and I don't want to know! If you think I am coming back to do this again, to feel this fear, you are wrong. I then realized that I was still shaking. What an experience this all was.

"Help me," I whispered, and looked at him with a sad face. I felt so vulnerable and naked. He looked and slowly started speaking:

"You have many beautiful gifts. Your connection with people is through other people's pain. You can see it, and it goes through you. That's what you are here to do. You have lots of pain inside you—that's why you can understand them, all of those people around you. You are a beacon of creation. But I can't help you... you need to heal your past, and not only that, to change your roots. You have to change the ground of your existence. And no one can help you with that. BUT LOVE IS THERE!"

I frowned.

"How can you live to see these THINGS on this Earth and still be here and feel normal?" I asked him, feeling disappointed. I felt my tears coming again. This session was getting so emotional for me. "I was suicidal one or two years ago," he replied. I felt both relief and release. This sentence was coming from his heart. I felt close to him. *I am not the only one here who has wanted to end this life.*

"So what did you do?" I asked automatically, ready for a magical recipe for how to live life with these ghosts around and somehow now stay alive, and not kill myself. "I prayed," he answered, and sat on the chair in front of me. He crossed his legs in a delicate way, one leg crossed over the other.

"You need to learn how to pray," he said.

I blinked, sitting there looking like a deer in headlights for a minute. In my mind, without saying a thing, I had certain thoughts. The first thoughts I had of prayer brought up old images of religion from my past. I grew up in the communist Czech Republic, where praying or believing in something else other than science was not acceptable. I thought of the moment minutes before when my grandmother appeared again. I remembered her stories about Buddha, Jesus, Taoist Masters, and other kinds of spirituality. They were beautiful bedtime stories, like fairy tales. She was different. She knew. She was me. I felt it. She was close to *it*—and whatever *it* was, I was beginning to understand it intuitively.

"All I can do is *try*?" I said, feeling sad. *So this guy won't make it go away... he's telling me I have to live like this? With these spirits around, which aren't from this world?*

Everyone wants to know things. But when you really know and see, you wish that you didn't—to know when someone dies, to feel it coming; to see colors around people. This is just crazy, I thought.

"See you next week?" he said, looking into his appointment book. "I have another person waiting outside."

Misa Art

"Hm... I will call you," I replied, thinking, *I will never call this guy. Is he crazy? I won't go through this again.*

"I have a feeling I will see you," he winked at me while I was leaving the room.

"How many ghosts can you see?" I asked instead.

"Oh, lots and lots of them around you! When you are a light you bring them to you, but one day after you turn them into light, they will help you. Because love is there," he smiled again.

"So I'm going to help a thousand ghosts turn towards the light?" I replied sadly. I didn't understand what he meant by the light and turning them from dark into light. At that moment I didn't know, but much later it would all come to me.

"You can give me whatever you have, I know you don't have money right now." I gave him my last fifty-dollar bill. "Thanks, buy yourself a beer," I tried to joke.

"I don't drink anymore, but in the past I did. A lot." He winked again at me, like he could tell my next move.

I closed the door behind me. «Pray,» he said. «Right..." *Ugh. Well, that wasn't the kind of help I thought I would get here.*

Tower of Light

I ran from his office, and refused to take the elevator on the way out. The last thing I wanted to feel was a bunch of people and their energy close to me. *I need a drink. I need a couple of drinks to forget about this and feel normal. I just want to feel normal.* Yes, I was always a little different—I saw ghosts when I was little, talked to white light-bodies that no one else saw—but everyone always thought it was just a child's imagination.

"She is just a child," people used to say.

My own mother was scared of me when I told her at five years old that I was *her* mother; that I would take care of her, mother her, and nurture her; that she doesn't need to worry. She smiled when I told her. But ten years later, when I kicked her abusive husband and my father out of our lives, she stopped laughing at the things I shared with her about spirits and realized that I know certain *things*.

But this shaman experience was a bit too much—even for me, as crazy as I am. I needed a drink. I dialed her number—my soul sister. She has dark eyes and a thin face, an Italian girl full of fire. She looks like Cher, and I look like a short Marylin Monroe type, with intense big blue eyes. *Those same blue eyes that scared so many people.* We looked like opposites, but were so close at heart and had a similar drive and similar intense energies. We both knew there was something that would hold us together, no matter what. We were always there for each other. *My best friend.* You need this when your entire family lives in a different country. *I need to talk to her, have a drink, and get drunk… then I will finally feel normal.*

Misa Art

"Hello, Hallloooo..." she yelled into the phone. "Are you there?"

"Yes, bambina, sorry, I was just staring at the wall." I made another joke to lighten the situation while I was running down the stairs. "I need a drink."

"Ok, got it. Emergency drink!" she replied with her kind voice. There was lots of noise in the background. She called it an "emergency"—no judgment, when we were in trouble or if there were many emotions falling into our hearts. She always knew, and could always tell.

"Are there troubles in your heart?" she asked. "I am filming right now, can I tell you more later? Just come meet me, we are on State Street!" We were in Chicago.

"I am coming! Then I have to stop by at my art show!" I was a visual artist, and she was a producer for her own production company. Filming—she was always filming. She reminded me of how we used to run with cameras and a crew around Chicago and New York, trying to save the world, filled with passion and ideas about how to make it happen. She was the gypsy, and I was the witch. We used to laugh about it. She was a strong personality, like me—very strong—and anywhere we walked, people would notice our power together. We always made people laugh and made them feel inspired. We were unbreakable. But now, in this moment, I felt like a lost little girl.

"Coming! I will be there in ten minutes!" I screamed into the phone, and hung up. I wanted to get inspired.

Tower of Light

I crossed the street in Chicago. People everywhere—and now, since the shaman's session, I began again to see the weird colors around them. The urge to have a drink was stronger than the temptation to stop and look. I didn't think I had a problem with alcohol. I knew as an artist, we all drink, we all have highs and lows, and we all just try to express somehow what is going on inside. So we smoke and we drink, and sometimes we die from it. I had a history of trying drugs. I tried all of them. I made notes of it in my diary in the Czech Republic as a teenager. I think I went to every rave party out there. I hitchhiked everywhere around Europe. I was seventeen at that time. I was still wondering why I didn't die then. I was always a free spirit—probably too free. Now I am thirty-three and still going full power into things. *Stubborn. That's how I got here*, that was the song I sang in my mind while crossing the street in Chicago.

Hot! Sexy! A man was standing there looking HOT! He was a model, actor, of course. My weakness—models and bottles—the weakness of "fake" beauty. I felt shallow to admit that I just loved to look at good-looking people. Shallow? My excuse was that I was an artist; everything was beautiful in my eyes, but hot-looking people just ignited this spark in me. They didn't need to talk; their look alone spoke for them. I smiled and walked behind the scenes of the filming shoot that was going on.

Misa Art

He was an actor, and on second glance I could see and read his aura. Yes, I could see the green chakra—the first time I could see these colors was when I was doing yoga once. I could see different colors around people. This guy reminded me of another model I had painted—a total artist's obsession. They had the same female energy. That was the time in Florida when I totally lost my mind. I did a huge show on chakra's energy. I can see the energy around people, and was totally in love with a model who had female energy. This actor guy reminded me of him. The guy I painted before was not necessarily gay, but I felt that he was still looking for himself. In the closet? Maybe. Who isn't in some kind of closet these days?

I am totally nuts. I pretend to be normal around people, but I see "things"—so it makes me feel like I'm in a spiritual closet. Sometimes I want to hide. I wondered at that time why I attracted guys who were more sensitive. Probably because I was strong; maybe too strong for "strong" alpha-male type men, who I would only fight with in my past relationships. So I picked men who were strong in emotional sensitivity. Maybe it was my own daddy issues—again, who knows?

I remember how the shaman said he was once suicidal. *Thank God I am not the only one here who's crazy.* The thought of him made me calm. But the feeling that I will die this year didn't go away.

"Hi, bambina!" My best friend winked at me from behind the camera. Her crew was listening to her. The model slowly looked at the camera—you could tell how much he loved it.

"Hey G, are we doing the drink?"

"Yes, we are almost done here" she whispered.

Tower of Light

The crew and the tall actor slowly started to pack equipment up. I moved closer to her and whispered,

"I met a shaman today."

"What did he say?" she asked, like it was a normal thing to meet a shaman in 2012 in the middle of a huge American city; as if it was a normal thing like going to a Walgreens to buy something.

"I will tell you later. He said, *PRAY*."

"Well, that's the truth… let's go to this event, and you can tell me more. Are you wearing this?" She pointed at my long dress, and didn't pay attention to my sad face.

"No, let's go shop for something sexy, I just want to feel sexy." Shopping wasn't usually my thing. Many people go buy "things" when they want to feel better, but someone once told me if you don't feel good, try to look your best because it will help.

I knew that the actor could probably hear me.

Misa Art

I said "sexy" a little loud—well, that's because he is sexy. He waved at me. *Yep, hot.* He was so hot. *Nah, I won't go there, not again.* I am divorced- my ex-husband cheated on me with my friend, and I ran away. Three years later, I had a deep soul-relationship with a great guy, but couldn't handle the possibility of living in New York. So, I ran again, and then I just ended up with another toxic. I called him "toxic." The toxic-one totally damaged any good ideas about relationships in my head. *Everyone meets a devil once in their life,* G used to say, *but never marry those types! Never ever! They will promise you things, then just destroy you.* It happened; it could happen again. He destroyed me. He never broke my heart, he just made my mind totally blurry; he broke my wings, and I started to doubt any guys out there who were "single and ready to mingle." The older you get, the harder it is to choose and trust men.

"Ok, let's go." Gina packed her cameras and put them into my car. We used to cruise around this windy city listening to loud music and never stop. It was our form of therapy. Off we would go around the town playing loud jams, moving with the music, and singing loud behind a steering wheel! We picked pretty sexy dresses, got changed, and jumped into the car again.

When we got to the party, it was huge! Bottles, models, and others who wanted to be famous were there. People say "smoking hot"—that definitely fit us that night.

Ugh, and now I have to act like I belong to this chaos of art, music, and fake smiles. But, I had to say, some lights and auras around people were nice. I slammed my first shot of vodka. *I don't want to see anything, I don't want to feel these people.* Gina was standing next to me smiling and talking to some man in a nice suit. He moved closer to me.

"Hello, is this your art? Are you the artist? You sold an art piece to Lionel Richie, correct?" he played shy, but his aura-color around him told me that he worked in the corporate world, that he struggled to act normal every day, that he had a wife at home, and that he was not really sure what this life is about. Money, his drive was money. *Cheap guy.*

I couldn't help it. I was judging him, but I was reading him also. I saw how he hurt people… he did. *Selfish.* "Yes, I am actually trying to be an artist!" It was his attempt at making a joke, at holding and hiding everything inside him, which I could read.

"Do you like this one? Why?" I asked. It was very interesting when people were standing in front of my art, not knowing why they even like it. But I knew. The story and time when I painted it connected with their souls; they were in the same situation. It was always on point; it always connected with their souls if they were affected in a deep way.

I slammed another shot. Everything started to feel normal. I didn't see too much distracting energy things around people, and could happily smile back at them and pretend. The night was about to get interesting.

"I like it, it reminds me… of something… of someone…" He continued talking, without picking up the clue that I didn't care.

"It's called *Frosted Ego*," I replied. I knew he wouldn't buy it—I can smell it miles away. He annoyed me. But I needed the money. I felt like a prostitute, but instead of my body, I was there to sell a piece of my soul.

"It's for sale you know, your wife would like it and your kid, too." He looked at me weird.

Shit, he never told me he is married with a child.

"I never told you I am married." *Well, then stop flirting with me and my friend and go home to your wife and kid*, I thought. *Another cheater.* I started to feel the heat in my cheeks. Gina saved my situation.

"Yes, but we can see things… we are women, women have a radar." She laughed.

I winked at her. "That's right." My tone was cold. The third shot of vodka went down my throat. I didn't care about this world, this art world, and people looking pretty—they just sucked everything out of you.

I am not going to do this, this is just torture for me. People are mingling around, looking at me and wanting to talk to me, but all I want to do is run. Run away, because I feel them, all of them. Their pain, their acts, their truth, their lies, when they will be hurt…

"Let's go dance," I grabbed Gina's arm and moved away from the crowd.

"Are you ok? You're starting to be a bit mean, bambina."

"No, G, I am not, ok? I just experienced a ghost party on my body a couple of hours ago in that shaman's office, and I am just not normal. No one can help me."

"Bambina, it will be fine, you will be ok." Her voice was full of hope and faith. "He said, *PRAY.*"

Tower of Light

My great friend tried to make me feel better, but I didn't listen. I didn't want to listen to anyone—I couldn't even listen to myself. I felt like I was losing my ground, I didn't know what was real and what was hallucination. *There is something wrong with me, and no one can see, no one. He did.* My thoughts went back to that little guy who called himself a shaman. But I resisted that feeling, the feeling of someone holding my hand and the voice of my grandmother. I didn't want to feel vulnerable. I closed my heart so that no one could get in.

"Well, I have no time for that right now. I need to sell something and probably should go home to Europe. I don't know, I don't know what to do. G? Some voice inside me makes me feel like I am going to die this year."

"No bambina, don't say that... just dance!" she grabbed my hands and started to move, and I moved with her. The groove of the music—yes, finally things started to be blurry and my mind was not going 24/7. I was drunk. Not "buzzed---drunk". I loved that blurry state of mind. I finally didn't have to feel or see anything. I was completely numb, far away from this world, on a cloud of alcohol blindness.

I didn't feel that I belonged to anything or anyone. I felt like I was on a cloud, like I didn't belong to this world when I was sober—but when I was drunk, I had an excuse. When you are drunk, nobody expects you to have clear feelings, you can stay on your cloud, and society will accept you. When you are on this cloud in a sober state of mind, they just look at you and think that you are crazy. Yes, I felt crazy after I saw the ghost party on my body today. *But there is Love*, the Shaman had said. *If there is Love, I just can't see it, because the smoke of ghosts around me is just too big.* We are blind, and we follow more blindness when we are not happy. I was totally drunk at this point.

1st Chakra

"The more you let fear win, the less understanding you have; fear will bring more dark shadows to your world."

"You are blind and self-destructive when you are in fear, or when you are not loving yourself."

"Alcohol and addiction offer a fast but temporary escape, and not a long-term solution."

"There is synchronicity, and there is an abundance of light no matter how dark things seem."

Chapter 2
Dreams of Predictions

Dreams of Predictions

I was driving down the street. The lights were bright. I was holding a steering wheel and listening to the sound of music. I got a text message on my phone. I grabbed it, holding my phone in one hand and the steering wheel in the other. I looked down and tried to reply—*grr*, couldn't get the text to send. I looked down and started tapping on the screen. I was still driving. Something in the street caught my eye—I looked up and slammed on the breaks.

!!!SMASH!!!

I saw his brown eyes for a split second—a boy. It was a brown haired boy, a little boy with a bicycle. I could hear the sound of a body hitting my car. *Too late—I killed him. I KILLED HIM!*

I opened my eyes. *Oh my God, oh my God*, I felt sweat all over my body, I looked around. I was sitting up in my bed. *I killed him… no, it was just a dream.* I held tight to my bed and sweat was dripping all over my body. This dream was real, a type of dream I have known since I was a little girl. You can feel everything in those dreams—the air, the smell, the colors. Those dreams are different. You can see everything through your eyes, not like dreams that feel like you're watching a movie. This was a prediction, a premonition; I felt it deep down in my core.

I got up from my bed and took a deep breath. *I will kill a little boy... I will have an accident and kill this boy.* I closed my eyes and could still see his face, his brown hair, his eyes—like a deer's eyes. He was so innocent. I dialed Gina's number and she answered immediately.

"Yes?"

I whispered into the phone. *"I will kill a little boy!"*

"What? What are you talking about?"

"I had a dream, I had a dream, that I will kill some boy—" I started crying. "I can *not* text in the car..."

"Okay, okay, calm down bambina, it was just a dream." She tried to make me calm.

I looked around my art studio. No one could make me calm. I knew it. I could still taste last night's alcohol in my throat.

"I have to go, thank you for listening... I will talk to you later."

I hung up.

I put my pants on and started to paint. I picked up my tools, my grinders, some wood, and started chopping like a maniac and moving to the music.

Tower of Light

His face won't go away... I needed to dance and paint, thinking that was the only way to get that face out of my head. I splashed the paint and let the music guide my painting, like a dance. *Music is the only way to stop my mind from going crazy...* I felt my sweat. I was still hung over from last night. *Splash, splash*—the sound of my paint-brushes creating new art. *I won't text and drive, I promise...* I whispered into the colors and then started talking to myself. "I won't text and drive."

Suddenly, I heard the sound of a whistle. Someone was whistling outside. It wasn't a hallucination, it was real.

"MISAAAAAA!" I turned down the music. It was coming from the alley.

"MISAAAA!" *Shit.* Yes, it was my friend's voice. I had no doorbell, and I had shut down all of my digital devices—when I paint I like to be alone, insane, with no distractions.

I stopped.

"YEAH?" I screamed back toward the open window to the alley.

I then had a flash of a memory—how back in the day I would get big paintings out by sliding them off the roof top, when I needed to. I bent over the edge of the old window.

"Yeah?"

"We have a photo shoot! Remember?" She screamed even louder.

My photographer friend was waving at me from the alley—Mary Carol.

"Shit, that's right!" I smiled. "I was painting. Sorry, I totally forgot."

"Ok, get your shit together and meet me by my car." She rolled her eyes.

I pulled myself out of the window. "Ok, but could you drive?"

"Of course I can, why?"

"Oh nothing, it's just that I don't feel like driving…" Somehow I pulled together another smile out of my face.

She waved again and started walking to her car. I looked around my studio. *Ok, let's get cleaned and take one last look at what I just painted.* I had created the Goddess - Zulu of Prediction. The face was looking at me from out of the painting with what felt like warning in her eyes—*is the universe warning me about something? Haven't I seen enough strange things by now?* I ran out of my studio to meet my friend downstairs.

"You have to move out of your studio?" Mary Carol asked me in the car.

"Yes. I have no idea where I will go. The landlord wants me to move, after all the money I've put into this place." I replied to her with a sad face.

"That totally sucks." She mumbled back. Mary Carol was driving too fast.

"Can you drive slower?" I held tightly to my seat belt.

"Ha! I'm only going forty—are you ok?" She winked at me.

Tower of Light

I told her about my premonition. By then we had arrived at the photo shoot. She smiled, while moving all of the cameras out of her car. She was tall, with brown hair, always very athletic—that's how we met, it was at yoga.

"We should get you some guy to distract you from your dreams," she spoke sarcastically, but was also serious. We left the car and walked through the makeup artist crew and models. *Distractions... we all want some distraction to move us away from reality.*

Those body-painting days... memories came into my head. *How many naked bodies have I seen in my life? Perfection. But what is perfect? The world of perfection and shallow fame—models and bottles, again. Blurry visions of perfect bodies in an unperfected world, bottles of alcohol, the fast-driven life—all to forget about this world, this unreal reality.*

"Nah, I don't feel like any guy will be able to take this dream away, to stop this madness of mine. You know? I went to see a shaman last week, and I saw stuff I'm afraid to describe to anyone. The world would think I am crazy. For now I can hide behind the "artist" mask, but all these things are happening—and then there's the dream of me killing a little boy. I have a feeling that I will die. What's happening to me?"

"Nonsense. You were depressed before. Do you remember your suicide thoughts when you went to Florida?" She said, moving closer to the crowd of models. Memories filled my mind as I followed her.

Yes. I had planned my suicide three months before. I had rented a house in Florida, packed my stuff, and planned my last art show. I had invited my mom and a friend from the Czech Republic, and then I simply didn't do it.

I couldn't. I imagined how my mom would live her life if her daughter simply just ended her life. Yes, I was mad at her. I never had the chance to be a child, always felt like my mom was my child. I couldn't go back on the promise I made to her when I was five—that I would take care of her, that I would be her mother.

I already live my life by myself, on a different continent from my mother. Although I loved her, I was mad at her. *She couldn't stop my father from being abusive.* I remembered how I had kicked him out of our life when I was fourteen. *I couldn't even kill myself, because she wouldn't survive that guilt. Probably any mother wouldn't survive it.* Yes, I planned it, but I didn't do it. I felt angry again.

Now I have a feeling that I will either kill a boy or I will die. I can't explain all my inner thoughts or visions. It is starting to be a bit too much.

"Yes, I remember, Florida was fun. But I think I realize that I am a functioning bipolar, without medications and visions of predictions. The shaman last week saw it all. I think I should see him again" I answered instead.

"If you think he can help you, do it." She was starting to take photos of the models around us—the perfect bodies.

I knew that no one could help me, that no one can help anyone—that the help is inside each of us. *But that old medicine man saw it, he understood me.* I felt compassion, which gave me hope. But I was scared, scared for what is coming. *Pray, he said... Pray. But how? How should I pray, and for what?*

Tower of Light

Not to have visions? Not to feel the world? Everything was coming through my body. *I just don't want to be so sensitive. I just want to feel normal.*

Maybe all I need to do is accept that I will never be normal. I'm tired of trying to seem or look like I am. I knew for some reason I didn't like myself. That feeling was coming from way back in my past, but I was constantly running too fast to see myself—to see who I really am. I was diving into the problems of other people to forget about mine. *I have a problem. I am not sure if I like myself and visions. It is a gift, but I don't freaking want it.* I closed my eyes in the middle of the crowd.

"Hi Misa! I'm the person who contacted you on Facebook. I bought your painting in Florida."

I opened my eyes. Her voice was calm. A middle-aged lady was standing in front of me. I saw her eyes—they were similar to mine, bright and blue. From the other corner of my brain, I saw a blink of information. My brain started channeling without me asking. I knew her, but I felt it was not from this time. Her aura had a pink color. It was blurry, but I knew her, from before—like way, way before. At the same time I was thinking about last night with Gina, and I wanted to have a drink.

"Hi, I am glad you have my painting," I said. I didn't want to discuss my artwork.

I was tired, but there was something about this lady. I looked around the crowd of models. Mary Carol was far away in the corner, discussing some photo shoot ideas.

Misa Art

"Do you know something about Native American Indians?" I asked out of nowhere. She seemed confused. "...not really, why?"

"Well, look at my eyes—they are similar to yours." I smiled at her. She was kind, I could feel her kindness.

"What is that supposed to mean? I just bought your painting... with my husband..."

"Well, we were in the same family... a while ago... I mean like, a *while* ago," I said.

She looked at me, confused. I knew I had only just met her in this life, but the feeling was so strong. *I want to tell her of the feelings that I have, but I need to tell her slowly... I have been having so many feelings lately.*

"How is your husband? Is he ok?" I could feel her pain. I felt it very strongly—it was deep. Her eyes got watery.

"He is sick," she answered slowly.

"Cancer. Lung cancer," I said. She looked at me, even more curious.

"Yes," she came closer to me.

"He is going through chemo, right?" I asked, but already knew.

"Yes. Who are you? My name is Sue, but who are you?" She got a bit scared. Just then she received a text on her phone. After she read it she got pale.

She looked at me again, then the phone, then me again.

"Can we have a coffee? This is just strange—my girlfriend from Miami just texted me. She is very spiritual. She just texted me and asked if I 'met the artist.' She said that she has a feeling that this person and I were in a Native American Indian family—in my past life?! I am not sure if I believe all of this," said Sue, very confused.

"Maybe you should," I said with a smile. I grabbed my coat and started walking to the door.

"Let's go!" I grabbed her hand and we walked away. I forgot to say goodbye to Mary Carol, but that wasn't important. I needed to talk to this woman. My intuition told me so—and for the first time in what felt like a long time, I listened.

Like a mother... She was a strong person, I felt I could trust her. *My soul mother.* I knew her light. We had a long conversation. I knew I would be in contact with her, I just could sense it. I went home tired, but happy that I met this person. *Sue, my soul mom.* She was giving energy to others, but not too much for herself. She reminded me of myself—she wanted to help others, but self-love needed to come back to her big heart. *Her husband will survive, I know it. I just know—and something big is in store.* And I was happy to tell her.

2nd Chakra

"Believe in your dreams—understanding them can save your life."

"When you are feeling blue, create."

"Angels and helpers can come in the form of humans. You will find out later why."

"There are always silent voices that speak inside of us like songs that play; our heart holds the music."

Chapter 3

Sweat and Fear

Tower of Light

Sweat and Fear

I woke up sweating again—the same dream. *I killed him again! The boy on the bicycle... again and again.* It had been going on for three weeks. I had been painting and trying to get rid of these visions. It wasn't working—the vision was stuck in my brain like gum on the bottom of my shoe, sticky and gummy.

It had been three weeks since I saw the shaman guy... I didn't want to go back to see those ghosts, but something caused me to pick up the phone and dial his number.

He answered right away. "Hello. How are you feeling?"

"Well, I am not feeling that great. Trying to sell my art, make money, and not kill myself," I tried to joke. "I was wondering if I can come see you, but can we be more careful this time?" I asked.

"It was the best liberating act we could have done. The fear of who you are needs to be brought out into the open. Maybe we can meet at a sweat lodge tomorrow, it will be good for you," he said quietly.

Misa Art

"I have no idea what a sweat lodge is, and I'm not feeling like I want to sweat more after the dreams I've been having," I answered slowly. I respected him, and didn't want to say no. I trusted him when there was no male in this world I could trust. I felt his care for this world and for souls. I felt safe. He was the "soul dad" I always wanted and never had.

I knew that my problem with guys was deep. I just couldn't trust them. When your own father abuses you, it is really hard to trust—yet somehow I felt guilty for having these memories of hate, abuse, and sleepless nights. I wasn't loved by the first man in my life, and I felt resistance to all the men in my life that came after. I didn't feel safe. I was scared that if I trust, they will destroy my love; they will leave me; they will hurt me. So I always run, run from them and far away, before any relationship could even begin to grow deeper.

"Ok, I will try… email me the address and time, and what I need, and I will try." I hung up. I was sitting in my studio and wanted to brush my teeth and wash my hair… *like normal people do. I have to make myself. I know this feeling of being empty. When it comes, you need to just get up and do all of the things like a robot. When you stop moving, that's when the brain starts spinning all those crazy ideas—ideas about the purpose of life, how to make money, what to paint, who to love—the feeling of loneliness. I could not let it happen, not again.* I got up fast and started to pack my stuff. *I am going to that "sweat lodge" thing.*

I am going. Let's try, let's try… I'll try whatever might help! I do not want to go on pills. I knew there was something wrong with the chemical reaction in my brain, but I refused to take any pills. *I just need to go and do whatever this shaman guy says.*

Tower of Light

I checked the email, put the address in the GPS, and started driving two hours away from Chicago. I packed a t-shirt, shorts, two towels, and lots of water, just as he said in the email. The highway road got smaller and smaller as it led me deep into the woods. The color of nature in the fall was beautiful—amazing warm colors.

I should do this more often... Being locked up in the concrete Chicago world wasn't doing it for me. The art world, shows, alcohol... I needed to drive, to be in nature. Driving was making me calm, but even then I could feel the impending fear of the unknown—and the dream of the little boy was still on my mind. I googled "sweat-lodge" before I left, and came up with all kinds of descriptions of "Native American healing"—and for someone like me, they were horrifying. I do not like dark, small places full of people—and sweating? *Oh my God...* Suddenly the whole thing didn't seem like such a good idea. I considered my phobia of small places full of people, but I was still driving. *I have to try! All you can do is try. No fear. Try. I just have no choice.* "It will be good for you..." I still could hear his voice on the phone. *I don't want to kill anyone...* again my mind was going a hundred miles an hour.

"If this will help my dreams, these visions, then I have to at least try it!" I tried to reason with myself. *I just need to try.* I saw a wood house in front of me on the side of the road. *This is it.* I parked my car next to some other SUVs, and I saw a middle-aged lady getting her bag out of her car.

"Hi, how are you?" *An American way to start the conversation.* I always wondered why people need to know immediately how someone is doing. I wanted to answer, "Shitty." She smiled at me first before I spoke.

Misa Art

"I am good, how are you? Actually, I am not sure if I am in the right place… is the sweat lodge thing going on here?" I asked.

"Yes, it is. It will be beautiful. Who invited you?"

"Tom. Tom, the shaman?" I answered. I hope she will not kick me out or put me on a list of the weird strangers, without me knowing anything about it. I was already freaked out a little bit to begin with.

"Of course, come with me."

I followed her inside the brick house. There were more people. I could count ten people, all ages—I was the youngest one, for sure. *These are the sweating pros*, I thought, laughing to myself.

"Hello, I am Misa…" the people were sitting around the table and configuring some kind of colorful ribbons with Tobacco, making little colorful bags on a rope.

They were very quiet. *I am too loud. I somehow don't fit here.* But I was used to not fitting into any world. So I sat down and looked at what they were doing.

"Where is Tom?" I asked an older guy next to me.

"He is coming. Hold on tightly to those ribbons, and make a prayer-bead for yourself." He handed me little ribbons, rope, and some tobacco.

Tower of Light

As an artist, this task was easy. I got quiet and started tying the colorful ribbons together. *Praying. Ugh, praying, here we go again.* I was thinking about my family in Europe, my friends, my broken heart, and losing my art studio. I had no idea how to pray. So while tying, I was mostly thinking about things that bothered me.

"Here, I am done." I smiled and handed them to the other older lady at the table.

"No, you need to have that with you for when we go inside the sweat lodge."

"Ok." Again I felt like a weirdo. *Oh well, I will try this.*

Suddenly the door opened, and my sweet little shaman's smiling face showed up.

"Hi Misa, you are here, welcome," he said. "Come with me."

I got up, along with everyone else. I was happy he was there. I changed into comfy shorts and a tank top. "Coming!"

Everyone was quiet as we walked into the woods behind the little house. The sun was going down. I saw a pile of wood built into a bonfire pit. Right next to it was a small teepee and two cow skulls. *My grandma had those in her summer house*—suddenly the scene felt familiar.

We stood around facing the unlit bonfire, with the little tent behind us. *So that's the sweat lodge.* They did some kind of ceremony throwing pieces of tobacco into the fire while praying. They were all very serious and quiet.

Misa Art

"You'll be next to me, close to the door of the sweat lodge, so you can leave in case you don't feel good—but you'll be ok," my shaman whispered to me the exact moment I had a thought of running away again.

"Ok," I said. *He is reading my mind, for sure.*

All ten people crawled on hands and knees into the teepee, which now seemed tiny, and sat in a circle. I crossed my legs and held the towel in front of me. A little beam of light entered the small place. The ceiling, which was made of blankets, was very close to my head. I felt a bit of fear, as I never liked small places. Everyone hung their little prayer bags above them, so I did as well. My shaman's assistant started to throw hot stones from the bonfire into a hole in the middle of the circle. I watched him put about eight stones before the hot air took my mind off counting. The thick air filled my throat, and I tried to focus to catch air. I started to feel hot and nervous. The little tiny door was still open.

I can run now, my mind was going again. I could feel the people in the circle—all quiet. They filled the hole in the middle with the hot stones and closed the door.

My shaman was next to me. *I hope I don't die.* It was dark. I was shoulder-to-shoulder with 11 strangers in a tiny teepee. *I must be totally out of my mind if I think this will help me.*

I started to feel uncomfortable—very uncomfortable. And *hot*.

His voice was very slow and quiet.

Tower of Light

"We are here to heal the spirits. The first circle will start now. I am thankful for every soul here…" he continued speaking. I couldn't see my body—but in the sweltering air I felt sweat on my body, dripping down my body. I could feel the body next to me, and slowly stopped feeling my own. It was dark. One by one they were talking. They were saying personal things—some of them very deep stories. Some of them cried. I had no idea what I would say when my turn came. It was so dark and so hot. I was slowly losing my mind. It was my turn. My mouth was dry, and I could feel my hot body. I felt like I was alone inside the womb of the universe, like a child in a mother's womb. So I spoke into the dark.

"I am here, and thank you. I am here to wish that all the people in this world will be happy. I am here to forgive my father." I could hear my voice, but didn't understand what I was saying. My voice was saying it for me. I didn't see my body, I didn't see anyone. It was beautiful to say something loud, something that was from so deep inside me. I spoke. Then I was quiet. I felt it was out, out of me into the dark and into those stones.

"Beautiful," my shaman whispered. I felt safe. *Safe in this dark place, where no one sees me, no one can judge me.* Everyone was there to heal; all of them were looking for answers. Then, like in a dream, they were singing—and I was singing with them. I couldn't feel anything, I couldn't even breathe, but I liked it. It was like being on the edge of myself. I sang with them. I closed my eyes and hoped that I would be able to breathe, but after a while I didn't care. It was so hot and dark that I stopped caring, worrying, or having any fear. I was simply *there* and listening to the sound of Native American songs. I felt tears coming. I felt hot, but relieved; relieved from something I couldn't understand.

Misa Art

After a while I saw an image of myself in Florida in that house I had rented. I saw myself planning my own suicide. It was six months ago. I had an art show and then I wanted to finish my life. I saw it, in my tears, in that dark sweat lodge. I cried again, and felt sad, that I could think about my life like that. But I didn't want to be in this world. Then I saw my mom, how sad she would be if I did it. I cried in that dark sweat lodge and felt relief at the same time. *Forgive me, please forgive me.*

The sweat lodge door opened. A beam of light came inside. The people inside stopped singing. More than four hours had passed, but it felt like twenty minutes. We crawled out, one by one. I felt very connected to all of them. I didn't remember their stories, but I could feel they were all very deep. I was very close to them. The cold night hit my body, and we all went back to the house. I had never been so hungry. I was soaking wet in my own sweat. My eyes were shining. I smiled at all those people. They gave me food, and they were all smiling. I hugged my shaman. I couldn't talk, but he knew. Somehow they all were suffering, and I felt safe in the middle of it all. They gave me food. They said goodbye, and I started to drive back to the concrete world. I felt clean and clear for the first time in a while. I didn't see the image of me hitting the little boy with my car.

Tower of Light

"Thank you," I whispered, "thank you," into the night full of stars. I realized that those stars looked like little sparks, just like on the stone inside the sweat lodge. I looked up and continued driving to the concrete world of Chicago. I felt like I left something in that dark sweat lodge… something heavy. I felt lighter in my heart, and I kept it deep inside myself. I forgot about the dream, I forgot about the fear and voices around me, I forgot how I wanted to end my life… deep down, I felt lighter. I smiled. After weeks of worry, I smiled for the first time. I was alone, but—for the first time in a very, very long time—I didn't feel lonely.

3rd  Chakra

"You should try everything that resonates with you."

"Don't be prejudiced."

"Nature is healing."

Chapter 4

Flying Geisha

Tower of Light

Flying Geisha

A few weeks had passed since the sweat lodge, and I had made a couple of sales. I paid my bills by painting custom artwork for clients, but I knew I would have to say goodbye to my studio. I didn't know when, but I knew it would be soon. Again, the "unknown" didn't help me to feel fabulous. I knew I had to move. I also knew that moving creates stress. I've moved seventeen times in my life. I took a deep breath. I was making some business plans with my friend, who's also a lawyer. I was supposed to sign a contract about my upcoming art business—to partner up with him. I was standing in front of this situation and didn't know if I should do it or not. It felt weird and risky—but I had no choice. At least, I thought I had no choice.

"I will decide after Halloween," I told him after he sent a five-page contract with the details of our proposed partnership. At that time I had no idea what was coming, because I had shut off my intuition about anything—along with my worries. When we worry, we can't see clearly.

"Let's go party tonight," my roommate said—half asking, half declaring. "It's Halloween! Come on, Misa."

I didn't feel like going anywhere, and had no desire to be around drunk people. I had been drinking a lot, and didn't want to get drunk again... I knew that I would only be drinking to forget about my financial and personal problems.

Misa Art

"I don't feel like it," I replied. "But I can body paint you, you know…" I moved the paint brushes in my studio and started to paint on her body and face. I painted her like a Mexican skeleton on the Day of the Dead—*Día de los Muertos*.

"Come on Misa, let's go, just for a bit!" She had convinced me by now, so I changed my clothes. I found a blue wig, two tree branches, and a kimono, painted my face silver, and decided that I would go out just for a couple of hours.

Halloween night started. The night was dark and heavy, the same as my feelings. For some reason I had a feeling that I wouldn't stay around masks and people in costumes, drinking tonight only so they could be hidden underneath their pain and usual masks. It makes them do crazy things. You can do crazy things when no one sees your face, it's easier. We can be "crazy" under the cover of masks.

We arrived at a small local bar. I was dressed up as the Blue Geisha—with no idea that, in just a few hours, I would be flying one. I felt safe in the idea that nobody could recognize me. I ordered a beer, some people were dancing, I was standing by the bar. I was in no mood to talk to anyone.

"Hey Misa, is that you?" It was my friend, a singer. A beautiful girl, she was; she smiled at me.

"*Pssst*," I said, trying to keep my identity a secret. "Yes it's me, how are you?"

"I am good. I haven't seen you for a long time, where have you been?"

Tower of Light

"I have been hiding, you know... I am not doing so well..."

I didn't feel like explaining the whole spirit, visions, shamans, and financial problems to her—even to her, a friend. I didn't want to share any of my "crazy mind things." So I looked at her and slammed down one beer, then another, and fast.

The whole bar felt weird to me, full of masks and dark shadows—it reminded me of my nightmares. I started to have the heavy feeling that I had been having, and again...

"I have to go, I just have to go. I don't feel well."

She looked at me, surprised.

"You just got here! Come on."

"No, I have to go." I grabbed my bag and started moving toward the door.

"I need some fresh air," I mumbled back at her. I walked outside quickly and dialed my phone. "G? Where are you?"

"In Amsterdam, bambina, filming some things... how are you? Happy Halloween!" She sounded so happy and beautiful. *Gina! Oh how I love her.*

"I am good... well, not so good. I feel something weird, Gina. I cannot describe it."

"I will call you later, I just have to walk."

Misa Art

I put my phone into my pocket and rushed across the dark street of Chicago. *I just need to get into my car and drive home... I don't like this night.* I felt heavy again, heavy and dark. I started moving faster, faster, just to cross the street—*there is my car... over there! Let's go Misa, just get home... but what is home anyway?*

Whoooooooooom, whoooooom, whoooooooooom, ooooohmmmmmmmm, whoooom...

It was dark. There was only this sound vibrating through my body. *Whooooom...ohhhhm... whooom...*

I felt so light. I couldn't see anything, just the vibration of light. I realized I didn't see or hear through my ears. I could only FEEL the sound. I could feel the sound inside my heart. *Open your eyes,* I thought—but I didn't have eyes. All I could feel was the sound. *Whoooooom, whooom—*

I realized I had no body. I had no hands or arms. I had no pain, no pain at all. *Wherever I am, it is so peaceful here.* I smiled. I felt the dark, the darkness again, first... then the sound again. I felt the dark, but I didn't see the dark—and it felt peaceful, so peaceful. *Wow, it is very powerful here. Where am I?* I had no idea, but I felt safe. It reminded me of the sweat lodge. *Am I in a sweat lodge? How did I get here?* I don't remember how I got here. From far away the beam of light starts shining, just like the door in the sweat lodge when the shaman opened the tiny door.

"I am in a sweat lodge!" I smiled. But I wasn't sweating. I didn't feel my body, or feel hot. I just felt profound peace. The sound stopped. The beam of light was traveling closer to me—closer and closer.

Tower of Light

Inside the beam of light was LOVE, loving LIGHT, and WISDOM. I wanted to feel it around me. *Come closer,* I thought, *closer, please come closer. I love you.* The light filled my heart, full; in that moment I received tremendous information about the light-world. All of it—suffering, sadness, and happiness—it was all injected through me. But I wasn't sad or in pain. I was happy, safe, and loved. I felt peace. *Oh my God, I want to stay here.* I had traveled the whole world, but this was my home. *I want to stay here.*

Whooooom, whooom... From nowhere the sound was back. It started to vibrate my body. *Whooooom, whoooom...*

"Noooooo! Hello?! I want to stay here!!!!"

I felt and saw huge, huge feathers around me—grey with dark tips.

Whooom, whooom...—the sound was powerful, and overpowering.

I want to stay HERE, I wanted to scream, but I realized I had no voice. Something picked me up, something loving and very powerful. I felt safe and protected. I could feel male energy—not a man, only the strong energy—he was huge and strong. I couldn't see him, I only saw the big feathers.

The sound changed into one sentence. That sentence went through my soul. I could feel my complete being—I could feel my soul.

"Now the ground—not the roots—the *ground* of your existence will change, so listen." This sentence vibrated through my soul with the sound. This sentence, which I heard before from the shaman. I started shaking. I started to feel my body... *my body, I have body again!!*

I could hear, from far away, the sound of ambulance sirens. The words filled my heart... I smiled. It was dark again. The beam of light was gone, but I felt SAFE and LOVED.

"She opened her eyes for a second... don't move her." I could hear someone's voice. *Pain. Cold, pain*—the pain in my head was strong.

"Hello, hello, do you know what happened?" The voice was talking to me. I was cold, and the pain in my head was sharp. I couldn't open my eyes.

"No," I whispered. I felt water behind my head, I could feel pain and I was cold.

"She doesn't know," the voice said. "You..."

"You were hit by a car. Don't move, just don't move."

The water behind my head started to be cold. I could feel the ground. I was lying on the floor in the dark... It wasn't the floor, it was a street. I blinked and saw people standing around. I saw a mask... *the mask of Death*. I could hear voices, human voices. I realized, it is not water, it is my blood! I moved my arm and touched the back of my head. Tried to move my palm closer to my face. It was dark and blurry. My whole hand was red. *Blood! I am bleeding.* I felt tired. The dark continued. *Sirens.* Someone was holding my hand. Dark again. *I will be ok. No worries, I know I will be ok*, I wanted to say back to them. The dark was warm, my body was cold, and I couldn't move. But someone was moving my body—it was a weak body. Ambulance sirens. Dark again. Nothing. *Nothing.*

"Hello, hello..." I could hear a female voice.

I slowly opened my eyes, and found myself in a white room with separated drapes. *Oh... softer than the street.* She was wearing a blue outfit. She was smiling.

"Hello. Don't move," she said.

I was lying on white bed sheets, on my right side. *I am in an emergency room.*

Ouch. Sharp pain in the back of my head.

"Don't move."

"I have a hole in my head, don't I?" I asked.

"Yes, a big one. Please don't move. We did your scan—you didn't break anything. We cannot believe that you didn't break anything, only the head. The right side of your body is bruised. You were hit by a car tonight." I looked down and my knee was triple sized. *Ouch.* I couldn't move it.

"Please don't move, we have to staple your head in a bit."

"Do it right," I smiled. I felt happy. With a huge hole in my head, I was smiling.

"The doctor will be right with you."

"I hope he is handsome," I replied.

Misa Art

"She is joking, she is back." I could see my roommate now standing by my bed, still body painted in the mask of Death. But I hadn't just seen the mask: I had met death itself.

The nurse smiled again and asked, "What were you tonight? We had to cut up your costume."

My "death mask" roommate answered, "Geisha. She was a Blue Geisha."

"Well, I was more of a Flying Geisha, I guess." I winked at her. I could feel the hole in the back of my head.

My heart was full of light. I couldn't tell them—I couldn't tell them where I was flying. I couldn't tell them what I saw. I knew the location was of my home, my *real* home. They wouldn't understand. I smiled. I still felt the information about this world. I looked at the nurses, helping people.... around them was a caring light. My roommate was glowing green light. *Wow,* I closed my eyes and *said, stop, stop.*

I opened my eyes and everyone looked normal again. *Wow, I have a switch... I can control this.*

The doctor walked in. *Handsome...* he was handsome. I turned on that switch inside me.

I could feel him. He didn't care about his job, he was not happy to be here. I didn't judge him. I had compassion for him—I knew why he wasn't happy. I could feel his whole life story.

"Move to the side, slowly..." he mumbled.

Tower of Light

"I am going to shave your hair a bit and then we'll staple your head. It's Halloween night, we are busy."

I could feel his energy. Nothing too exciting, but I didn't judge him. I felt light for everyone in this world. I knew at that moment why I am here. *I have so much to do. I am back.* I felt so happy. *I have so much love for this whole world.*

I smiled at him anyway. He put the heavy surgeon's staple gun close to the back of my head. *Snap, ouch. Snap, ouch...*

"That hurts..."

"I know, twenty metal staples... just hang in there."

"In two weeks, come back and we will take them out."

In the USA, emergency rooms are fast—you're in and out. I couldn't walk, the right side of my body was hurting; as for my knee, I couldn't stand on it.

My friends drove me home after they pushed me in a wheelchair. I was quiet and happy—so happy to have this light inside, this peace in my heart. I couldn't describe it to anyone, so I just smiled. I tried to remember where I was three hours ago... I couldn't recall the memory of it. I tried to remember what happened four years ago. I couldn't conjure any memories. All I could remember was the light, the peace, and the sound—the strong sound—and feathers... But I was not scared that I didn't know. I was happy, because I felt tremendous information about love and light, straight from the source. I felt like a different person, with a different heart and twenty metal staples in my head.

Misa Art

My friends gave me a bath at home. My family are my friends, since my family lives in Europe. They all came one by one. They were scared. They had heard that I was walking on the street on Halloween and got hit by a car, and the car had left me on the street, bleeding from my head. A couple of them described what had happened, how it was a bit weird that I had suddenly walked out of the bar by myself, how they came looking for me… how five minutes later, they all saw the ambulance coming and me lying there, bleeding from my head. No one saw the accident or knew who was driving the car.

I made a walking crutch out of a guitar stand. My head was pounding, and half shaved. I couldn't really walk. I couldn't sleep on the right side of my body or head. Every now and then, I had vertigo and I was puking in the mornings—but I could feel peace and still felt the sentence, and the voice.

"Now the ground of your existence has changed, listen."

I didn't want to tell anyone, since I am a person who never asks for help. Ever.

"Misa, you have to ask who did it. Post it on Facebook. Maybe someone was there, and people will pray."

My friend's voice—a very spiritual person—was talking to me on the phone.

"Ok, I will write something, I will call my family too. But I don't want to scare anyone. I am ok, I am so ok that I cannot explain…"

I wanted to see my shaman friend badly. I wanted to see him; I knew he would see.

Tower of Light

I posted some sentences about my accident on Facebook, but nothing really like "Look I am a victim of hit and run and have $40,000 in hospital bills." Because I didn't feel like a victim. I felt that I gained something so beautiful from this broken, stapled head of mine. We all can gain something very beautiful from very terrifying things. I knew.

I just wrote that I am thankful, that I am here, and if someone was there that night, to let me know.

"You are lucky that you didn't get *expired*." The police officer on the phone was really cold.

"I know, sir, but I am just asking about the cameras, etc., on the street and what actually happened. I have hospital bills that I am not able to pay… that's all, that's all." I knew we wouldn't find him, I knew we wouldn't find the guy who hit me with a car at fifty miles an hour and left me there. I knew no matter what, I would be ok. I felt so protected. I felt strong, even though I looked like shit and didn't have any money to pay my hospital bills. I knew it would all be ok, now and forever.

"Ok, here is the number of the detective you need to call."

I tried to dial the number, but then realized that I could not see the numbers—they were jumping in front of my head. *Shit, I cannot read numbers.* I concentrated and one by one I pressed the numbers. No answer. I left a brief message. My head was hurting so badly, but my heart was full of love for this world—I was in total peace. I knew why this happened. I felt not broken for the first time in my life… with a half-shaved head, twenty metal staples, and a limp, I was so in peace and so happy. I felt totally complete.

Misa Art

I felt no fear. I had lost the last fear: the fear of Death. I still felt the sound, light, and the peace, and how all of them together were beautifully spreading inside me. I felt "him," the protector—the protector who picked me up and took me back. I saw his feathers in the morning when I couldn't move the right side of my body. I could feel him standing behind me when I was making myself tea. But when I turned, nothing was there. I could sense him. He was still watching me. I loved him unconditionally, and felt his unconditional love every day.

I started to heal fast; I could feel people praying for me, I could feel the power of their prayers. I felt so strong inside because I knew why this happened to me, I just couldn't tell them. I knew my journey would be long. I could feel my purpose. I knew who to talk to first—my shaman. But I had to call my mom in Europe. After a couple of days in my apartment I first took time to shower by myself and put on make-up. I moved my hair to the side, so you couldn't see the staples in my head, and dialed her on Skype.

"Hi Mommy." She was sitting in front of her computer.

"Hi Misa, how come you didn't call for a week? What's new?"

"Hmm... there is something I need to tell you, but promise me you won't be scared."

"Oh my God, what happened again?" I knew I was always some kind of trouble child. I could feel my love and care for her. She was glowing pink, caring and loving.

"I love you so much, mom. I had an accident, but everything is fine... this world is so beautiful and I just don't miss anyone. I cannot describe it, but I don't even miss you; I know you will be with me always."

Tower of Light

"Oh my God, Misa, what happened? What are you saying?"

"Mom, I cannot describe it. I was hit by a car, and I am back. I am so happy and I love you so much. So much."

Her face was confused on the Skype screen.

"I am ok, I think I had some different experiences during the time…"

"What time?"

"Well, there is no time, time doesn't exist. But it was a hit and run accident, and while I was in an unconscious state I saw beautiful things… a different kind of consciousness. I felt the love of the whole world, I cannot describe it in words. I just know *things* now." I smiled at her.

"Are you ok?"

"I am. I cannot walk right now, I have staples in my head, but I know that all will be how it should. I saw my angel, I felt God, I think… I think we can call it *GOD*."

"Misho, I hope that your head is ok…"

"Mom, my head and heart are better than before… I just know that I should go on this journey. I have to."

The phone started to ring in the other room.

"Mom, I have to go, I think the detective is calling me. They are looking for the guy who hit me with the car."

Misa Art

"Oh my God, did you switch your health insurance?"

"No." I felt how she started to worry.

"Yes, I have $40,000 in hospital bills, but I just know I will be ok… everything will be ok… the light up there *told* me."

I left her on the screen and picked up the phone.

"Hello, hello?"

"Hi, is this Misa?"

"Yes."

"This is detective Henley. We have your case, but unfortunately there were no cameras on the streets, so it will be difficult to get more details."

"Well, thank you… can you just tell me who found me?"

"Yes, we know the person who stopped the traffic and called the ambulance."

"Can I have his number please?" I grabbed a piece of white paper and wrote the number that the detective gave me.

"Thank you so much for your help, I truly appreciate it. I wish we could find him to pay my hospital bills, but that is ok. I am not worrying."

I hung up the phone and dialed the number on the paper. The phone was ringing and I had a feeling of being so thankful, so thankful that I could breathe, that I could see; I was so thankful to be back on Earth.

"Hello."

"Hi, my name is Misa, I am the one who you called an ambulance for five days ago... the one on the street, you called the ambulance?"

"Oh my God, oh my God, you are alive! The police didn't want to give me any information about you. How are you?" His voice was surprised and happy.

"I am fine, I just would like to thank you for being so kind, so kind... I just wanted to say that. I am an artist and I will paint angels from now on."

The man on the other side of the phone started to cry. He cried, "Oh my God! You were flying in the air, I was watching from behind the black car that hit you... I saw your body fly over the top of the car, and then he left... I thought it was filming because it was Halloween. You know, and you were in that costume. But you were not moving and no one was there... I stopped the traffic and ran to you with my girlfriend. You were bleeding from your head..."

I had tears in my eyes. I started to cry with him. I didn't cry for me, I cried with him; I could feel his heart.

"I just want to tell you that I have a daughter, she is your age, and I was always fighting with her—and when I saw you on that street and held you, while you were unconscious, I promised myself I would never fight with her again."

Misa Art

"That is so beautiful, thank you, thank you for my life… I will never be the same." I knew he wasn't the one who gave me my life back; that he was sent there to get his own lessons and to learn. But I thanked him anyway.

I hung up the phone. My heart was full of love, and I was happy that this accident had happened.

Then, from nowhere, the image of the boy and bicycle appeared in front of my eyes—that nightmare, that premonition of the young boy from a couple of weeks ago, came back.

I felt a pressure inside my eyes, and knew: I knew that I had to be hit by a car to be stopped by a higher force. I knew this was the only thing that could have stopped me from driving and killing that little boy, just like in my dream. I just knew. I wasn't sure if I was the little boy, or if I was stopped from killing him, but I had a huge feeling inside my heart that all this actually happened in order to protect me, not to hurt me. It would give me something that I would not know until later.

"Thank you." I looked up to the ceiling of my apartment and put my hands into praying position. I prayed. I prayed for the first time in my life—to angels, to light, to humans, and to the Earth. I closed my eyes and imagined the beautiful light I had felt while I was lying alone on that street. I felt the light again in my heart. I started to vibrate… I started to vibrate with beautiful peace in my heart.

I felt love for myself. I felt love inside me going to all of the corners of the world. I felt the unconditional love which helped me to be back in this world. I was LOVE.. I felt that each and every one of us is love, and that we are all loved and protected by beautiful light, and that nothing in this world is an "accident." Nothing in this world is circumstance. I felt that every piece of the Earth is a piece of us. I felt that even the stars are a piece of me, a piece of everyone; that the power of *being* is so powerful, and that we as humans are so powerful. I felt that the power was coming through us into that unconditional source. I felt that light, and Jesus and the Buddhas and all of the saints are connected to it, and we are them and we are *it*... I felt the beautiful warm feeling inside me in that moment of happiness, and cried—I cried from love. I cried and released love into the air as I took my breath.

I felt, for the first time, thankful for all my gifts, for all I know, for all I don't. I felt peace. And I saw children—children and generations of pure energy that we are not responsible for, but we should learn from. We are here to learn so many things. And I saw patterns we should cut out, that we should start to be in the present moment. I understood the being... of the whole human light. I felt lighter. I felt happy. My eyes were brighter, and I wanted to stay in that moment forever. I saw layers of energy—the levels of consciousness. I knew I would never be able to describe in words what I see, feel, or know of this world on Earth, but I saw that I would build something very close to it. I saw that I wouldn't have a "normal" life. That was not why I came back. I saw I will build back hope for people—not through me, but through the Source which I had experienced. I saw the whole journey of it—the resistance—but at that moment I knew I would build something for humanity.

Misa Art

Later on I realized—that moment was my awakening. Awakening, not my second chance. It was the beginning of *me*, my true self, and I saw why I came back. I accepted the fact that this world would not understand, but that the "other" world would force me to bring this love to the Earth. I realized I wasn't scared to die. I realized that I want to *live*—after planning my suicide a couple of months ago, or deleting my memories, I was free and I wanted to live. I realized I didn't have a fear of the thoughts of society, my family, or any other humans in the world. I realized I had no fear of failure—I realized I had no fear. I knew and accepted who I am and what I have as a gift, and what I have to bring to this world from the other world. I understood that the journey would be my personal and, at the same time, global consciousness. I just knew, but the knowing wasn't coming through my head or brain—it was coming from my heart with green light.

4th Chakra

"To accept the gift sometimes means reconciliation—that this world might see you as a crazy person."

"There is proof of life after life."

"Sometimes you really have to be "hit" to "awaken.""

"The light inside has always been there. This light is the ground of our existence."

Chapter 5

Angels and Prayers

Tower of Light

Angels and Prayers

I dialed my shaman's number. *"Shaman's number," haha! It sounds so funny when you think about it. Everyone wants to call the shamans, and I have the phone number of one of them.*

"Hello? Misa?" His voice was warm, the same as I remembered.

"Hi, can I stop by your office?"

"Sure, what happened?" I knew that I didn't have to tell him—he could feel me. He knew how to *channel*. Channeling was something I could finally understand. The moment you concentrate on another person's energy—you think of them, they think of you, no matter where they are—and when you are really open, you can feel them. Many times, you can feel how they feel. Now I knew, and I had that switch; I could switch my spirit-awareness on or off if I wanted to. I had powers.

"I was hit by a car, many things changed… I know you are the one I need to talk to. I just know… it is so deep. So, see you in a bit."

I walked slowly, closer and closer to my car. After ten days, it was the first time that I was on the street. The sound of the cars passing by wasn't pleasant. I tried to not concentrate on my limping walk and the twenty metal staples in my head.

Misa Art

I drove very slowly. I felt like everything was new. I could feel the ground on the streets; I could see people and love all around. I was very calm inside, and somehow on the right side of the back seat I felt my angel. He was there—his silhouette was huge. I still could feel him...

I loved him unconditionally. It didn't surprise me that I felt him. On the way I stopped by my art studio to check on my birds. I walked close to their cage and I saw a little body on the bottom of the cage. I knew he had died, but I wasn't sad. I picked him up and said a prayer. I didn't know any prayers, I just used the words that were coming from my heart. I moved his body into a little box and put it into the ground behind my art studio. I thanked him again. *Thank you*. Instead of being sad, I felt love. I felt like he died instead of me. I felt I was connected to him. His little partner in the cage was looking for him, so I spoke to the bird and said, "I will bring you new life, a new partner, do not worry." I knew where he went; I knew the place. I knew he had to go. I understood the whole circle of life. I put ground over the box and smiled.

I drove slowly to the shaman's office and was singing a beautiful song on the way. It was for the bird, it was for his partner... I was celebrating death instead of grieving, but could understand the compassion felt by souls who didn't have the experiences I had, and don't know that they will see their loved ones again. Even the remaining bird in the cage would see his lost partner one day. I could feel it.

I opened the door of the shaman's office. He was sitting there, just like the first time I saw him. *My urban looking medicine-man.* This time I saw a huge light coming from his heart—green and calm. I turned on my hidden "switch." He smiled, but then I saw surprise in his face.

"Wow, the past is gone, your ground changed... and you have a huge hole in the back of your head!" He said it with lots of humor. He knew I was different.

I laughed. I was relieved that I could actually talk to someone who "sees."

"They are helping me, I feel them... Two on the back of my head blowing the love force from all the people who are praying for me, I feel it... I am healing so fast." I was talking and smiling.

"I saw my grandma, too, during the accident. She was wearing a very fashionable white robe, of course she was. Even in the other levels after death, she would pick the coolest outfit," I joked.

"I feel like my past is about my father and everything is a book. I am not attached emotionally to my past; all of my heartaches are gone. I feel so free and new."

He smiled kindly and came closer as I continued talking. I wanted to tell him everything... *everything*, like a little child with a great discovery.

"But what do you think about the spirit on the right?" I whispered, and pointed behind me at the air, though there was no need to whisper. I felt like I was connected with the divine masculine (my twin-flame), my entire soul... with no words, he was my other half; the aura of the man with huge wings on the right side was my other half. It was all there in the vision that I received during the accident.

"Wow, I can't see his face, but he is huge... and strong," Tom replied.

Misa Art

If anyone in this world would have been listening to our conversation, they would have thought we were totally crazy—a sixty-year-old man talking to a thirty-three-year-old blonde about spirits like it's a conversation about today's weather.

My medicine man was my spiritual father, I knew it now. I started to understand that everyone in this world, not by their blood but by their soul connection, can create families. Anything or anyone you are missing in your life, or is not in the position to be the right soul—brother or sister, father or mother, soulmate or friend or partner—you can call and ask for. What you seek is seeking you. The "calling" works. They are here on this Earth; if you ask or wish or pray, they will appear in some form. It is all here, and you will find them. Just ask. I realized how I manifested this spiritual dad. I realized that there is no good, or bad; I realized that everything is connected for better things. I realized that only if you are patient will it come.

"You are happy to be back. You are happy to be back in this world and on Earth. I am so happy for you." He sat down next to the angel painting and moved his massage table close to me.

"Yes, I know I don't have to explain to you what I saw, I know you see... I know why I am back, and I know now why I feel and see all that I see."

Tower of Light

"I am no angel, I know my other-half is on the astral level. He is the one with grey wings whose ends are dipped into dark. I know I am not perfect; I know I am half of everything and I know I am only human; but I know that I won't change whatever changed me, I will only try to change the view of others or help others to see the light. I feel it. I love me. I feel the power in my heart. I am love, I feel the light, every moment I concentrate on it… I know that this world is trying for us to forget who and why we are here, but the light is in all of us. We cannot forget. We all are LOVE. I didn't want to sound cheesy, I didn't want to sound weird—but the light was glowing inside me and I could resonate with it. It was the melody of my soul. I wish for the whole world to feel it.

Once again my medicine man put me on the massage table and was holding me on the bottom of my spine and head. He was doing cranial sacral treatment. He knew that I physically couldn't sleep on my right side and had vertigo and vomiting every morning. He sang again. I felt safe and loved. The visions of him holding me in his arms appeared, I knew I was in his arms before; not in this life, but in those lives before. The vision of me having a male body came, and he was holding me— we were somewhere in the middle of woods in my vision, and I felt tired—my body felt very tired, but safe. I knew I had died in his arms before. I opened my eyes and looked on the wall in his office. This was my first time here on this Earth in a female body, and that I knew. We all are looking in this life for the vibration of our soul.

Misa Art

Each of us has a different one. To meet someone with a similar vibration is also something we are looking for. I knew the sound I heard when I left my body, and I knew I would start looking for that sound all my life. I knew that the sound would come again—when I leave this world. I knew that my guardian was part of me, is always with me... I could still feel him. But I knew it wouldn't be soon that I would see him in full vision. We can only see them in full vision when we won't be returning back to this world. The session ended, and I had to go to meet my future business partner and talk about my art, space, and money, and deal with the physical part of the world. I needed to start working and talk to people and find a place to live, figure out how to pay my hospital bills—but somehow I felt this peace, I knew I would be ok. *All of it will be ok*—I could feel it in my future, and I couldn't describe it to anyone—that at the end, nothing is under our control, we all just think it is. Even though I would have loved to stay in the peaceful place in my medicine man's office for ages, I knew it was time to go. We never want to leave when we feel so good, but I knew we are always with those we love. I smiled and sat up.

"Come with me to South Dakota to see a Native American shaman, my really good friend Ed. Me and a couple of writers are going up there. Come!" my Shaman asked me after I got up from the table.

I closed my eyes and could feel the future road and travels. I could see my journey—I could see all that was coming for me to understand more of what happened to me, for people and this world. I knew my journey was not in the middle of a city, at parties or drinking, which I used to practice so well to forget about my pain. I didn't feel like having any drinks. I felt like I didn't need one.

Tower of Light

"Yes, I will go with you next week."

"Ok, see you then! We will drive there. Eleven hours, back and forth."

He grabbed a picture from his office wall and gave it to me—a picture of a standing angel. It was a beautiful painting, where the mother-angel with a middle-aged child was standing by a crib and leaning above the little baby angel.

He spoke softly:

"They all are powerful, the soft ones, the warrior ones… all of them. It is like us, growing from the baby into an adult. But their size or age doesn't matter; they all have the same light.

"You are like the baby now, cleaned, and taking baby steps toward wisdom and truth. Your journey is *now*, and all of the ghosts and spirits and angels will help you to see why—why you had to go through heartaches, betrayal, and problems, in order to open your heart to the spirit-world."

I was quiet. I knew now that listening was part of me, which I didn't do before—but I knew that in silence the truth from wisdom-souls is brighter and I can channel it better.

Listen, listen... I could hear the voice inside me. I hugged him again and thanked him for all of his gifts, and with my limping walk, shaved head, and an angel painting in my hand, I left his office. I started walking down the hallway of the high-rise building, back into the "real world" called Chicago. I felt the ground and my secret switch, which I could switch on and off between the worlds. But this time I wasn't upset about being a bit different. This time I felt the light and knew—*I am never alone. We are never alone.*

The fear of loneliness was gone. The bright light was in my heart, and my guardian was behind me. I knew I would be facing the real world and would have to be careful how much I share with the world, so they would not be scared of the truth. I knew that this world might not be ready for the truth, but that I would slowly find a way to bring the light back here to them. The human heart needs hope, needs faith in good things—it is the only way to survive in this whole world of "acting," society, and suffering. I felt strong, because I could still feel the light. *I cannot ever forget.* "Please don't let me forget, always show me, always remind me... in the coming times of my blindness," I spoke to myself, but knew that when I think or speak to myself, that I am heard by the light, by the saints, angels, connecters, and for sure by the one huge grey (spirit) behind me. I call that PRAYING.

5th  Chakra

"It is important to have someone with similar spiritual experiences and compassion. There is always a person who has similar experiences in this world."

"Everything that is alive in this world has a soul."

"You can call your angels anytime."

"Everyone is seeking the vibration that most resonates with their soul. That vibration is the song of the universe, which is love. When we hear the music, we spontaneously experience our souls to be dancing; those who cannot hear the music, look upon those who are dancing as crazy."

Chapter 6
The Power of Manifestation

Tower of Light

The Power of Manifestation

"Please, I won't speak on the phone. You know you stole them."

I was calm on the phone with my future business partner, who would not hold that title for very much longer.

"Misa, I don't know what you are talking about…"

"I saw the picture, the one you deleted from Facebook. Your wife is pregnant, and she posted a selfie. I saw the painting behind her. I never gave you that painting. I checked the inventory… there is more missing." My voice was calm, but I could feel the energy of my heart… *betrayal*. "Anyway, just stop by the studio."

He hung up and I drove to the studio. Two weeks had passed since my accident and I was worried that I had forgotten how to paint, because I had basically no short-term memory and no sense of direction. *Good thing I have GPS…*

Misa Art

This was a day before I was supposed to be signing the contract that would bring me out of my financial problems, to start a metal art business with my friend who, I just found out, had stolen some of my paintings. I didn't feel like crying. I knew this had to happen to keep me out of that business. I took it as a sign. I started to take everything as a sign—and more importantly, I started to LISTEN to the signs. The hospital started calling me for money from the accident, I was broke, and I had no idea what I should do—but I always closed my eyes and felt the light.

"I won't say anything to anyone in public, because I could ruin you... and because you are having a child, who will need a good father. But please don't contact me. We are done."

My no-longer business partner was standing in my art studio with one painting in his arms, all confused and listening. He did steal them.

I continued.

"Please keep the rest of them, as a gift."

"Misa, are we ok?"

I smiled. "I am not sure, but be well and take care of your kid."

I channeled his heart and wished him well, but at the same time I felt sad for him because I knew what could happen to people who steal or hurt others. I had seen it all up there during my accident. *Karma... that "karma" thing.*

Tower of Light

I couldn't look in his eyes, because I was upset that my friend could do something like that, but I took deep breaths and remembered the light. I knew that this happened only for me to see, to learn that this metal business wasn't the right path for me. It may have been lucrative, and of course I wanted the money—money can have great power when it's used for good—but my reality was different. I saw children I wanted to help. *It is not a metal business*, my inner voice whispered.

"Good boy." I closed the door behind him and knew I would not think of this as a crime or of myself as if a victim. I looked up behind the door and whispered, "Please forgive him"—and never saw him again since that day.

I was a bit tired, and looked around my studio. I knew I would have to say goodbye pretty soon... *no money, where I will go?* I picked up a brush and started painting. I painted an angel, the one I had seen on the street. I knew that I would never sell this painting. It was made to be given to my soul father. I started to dance in the middle of my art studio—*I didn't forget how to paint!* That realization made me happy, and I had no desire to drink. I came back home tired that night and slept very, very deeply.

Close to the morning—around 4 a.m.—I heard a noise coming from the back of my apartment. I pulled my blanket closer to me. I could feel a person in my apartment, walking into the kitchen and back.

I stayed in bed and watched my bedroom door. I knew what was going on.

Misa Art

I focused on the bedroom door, willing it not to open. I heard the noise again. After fifteen minutes, I got up and walked to the kitchen slowly. My computer—along with all the work I hadn't backed up to the cloud—was gone. Someone had robbed my apartment while I was in my bedroom. I took a deep breath. I had no computer, and all the digital pictures of my artwork were gone.

I was upset, but again, I told myself to listen. *Why is this happening to me? To forget my past completely? To be on the street with no money, in a different country?* I touched the metal staples in the back in the back of my head. My knee was starting to bend better, and every day I was giving myself yoga sessions—I had no money for physical therapy. I was starting to walk better; the metal staples would be taken out of my head in a couple of days. That day I filed a police report about the robbery and started to calm myself down. I sat in a yoga position with my wounded, swollen leg and closed my eyes. I didn't pity myself. I started to see the light again, and all the suffering in this world. Human lights that were going through diseases and cancers, children who were born with bigger problems than mine; I saw it all while I was channeling the suffering of this world. I saw that the Earth was crying, and my body started to vibrate... again, I concentrated on that light.

"Please, if you are doing this, just show me—just show me what I should do, and please send me help." I concentrated on the light in my heart and started talking to myself quietly.

Two days after the robbery, I went to see my photographer friend, Mary Carol. I was sitting in her apartment with a couple of other people.

Tower of Light

I didn't drink. I didn't need it anymore. I just enjoyed the conversation about art and other things. One of the group members sat next to me. "Hey, what's your name?" he asked me.

Nice, kind heart. I could feel him. I turned on my switch.

"Misa. I am Mary Carol's artist friend. What do you do?" (Usually I don't ask people first what they *do*, I ask them what they do for *fun*. That's usually more interesting, especially with those who are trying to be someone or something important.)

"I am a personal injury lawyer." When he said it, it was clear why I met him. He was sent to me. I understood then how this world works, how the asking and calling for help works; how we meet people, and for what.

"That's great, I just had an accident."

I described to him all of what had happened to me. He took my information and within two months, he had filed my case and all of my hospital bills were paid.

Misa Art

I started to concentrate on that light every morning and every night. I tried to see everything that happened from the perspective of goodness and love. I was alone with no partner and no financial help, but I wanted to help others with my experiences. Somehow I knew that things would be ok; the light was still there in my heart, peaceful. I said "thank you" every day into the air above me, behind me; I said "thank you" into the light. I said "thank you" when I saw the sun in the morning. I said "thank you" when I saw the grey spirit behind me. I was saying "thank you" so much that, sometimes, tears came from my eyes... they were so warm I knew they were from my heart, and that light. I was thankful—I finally could say that I was thankful. And I knew that those words were not only being spoken for me—I knew that they were being heard.

"Ouch, ouch!" I was sitting in a doctor's office in the middle of a hospital. My head was bent over and some cute nurse was taking the staples out of my head. Two weeks after the hit-and-run, my head was almost healed.

"Should I keep them, for good luck?" I joked while I looked down into the small bin full of staples, but the pressure while she was pulling them out was unbelievably intense.

"I can handle any pain, although I would always prefer physical pain over the pain in my heart that I used to have," I winked at her. I could channel—*she understands*. She smiled and called the doctor to check on the "artwork" that she was creating in my skull. I saw everything as art now.

Tower of Light

"So how is your sleep? You went through a trauma, you were in an unconscious state, head injury, in a hit-and-run accident." The doctor was holding a piece of paper and reading my hospital file.

"I sleep well, but I have to sleep on one side of my body otherwise I get vertigo... but all is good," I answered her with a wide smile.

"Do you have any memory loss? Forgetting stuff, etc.?"

I wasn't sure if I should start to talk about the light above me, about my visions of the world and of angels... I thought for sure she would send me to the "nuthouse." If I told her about me—that I was a a functioning bipolar, that my best friend was depression, that in dark times I had been planning my suicide, that I was seeing ghosts—she would surely insist on giving me some "magic pills."

"I feel happy, all of it—everything from the past—is just like a book. I don't feel sad. It's not so much a sense of direction, but I do know where I am going..." I smiled at her again. She was very serious. My smile just didn't work with her, but I kept smiling at her anyway. I saw her own pain, and her problems in her marriage. *She won't smile, not today.*

"Well, I suppose that lots of people, after traumatic experiences, feel denial as to reality as they currently experience it. We kind of do that as humans; we are trying to delete memories that don't serve us." She answered and looked at the file again. She was speaking from her own experience. I knew; I knew that she just couldn't see mine.

"So, you are feeling ok?" she asked, closing the file. She moved on to the other "case" next to me, not paying any more attention to me.

"Yes, I am feeling like never before. I'm doing my own physical therapy/yoga. I am totally recommending it to everyone. Magic." I winked at her and sat up while moving my growing hair to cover the scar on my head. *Science.* I knew it was not the case that science could heal me. I knew no one can heal anyone. I knew all of it depends how we feel in our hearts, how we see things, and how happy and positively we feel the light. My faith had nothing to do with religion or science: it was faith in that pure LOVE. But I respected her knowledge and education.

I gave her a hug. She needed it more than I did. She was surprised and quiet. "Thank you," I said. I left her standing there and saw, finally, a smile in the corner of my vision when I was leaving her office. *Her first smile today. She felt my light… not the science, but my light.* I knew she could feel it. She could deny me or not understand me, but she could feel it. That I knew.

While I gave her that hug, I imagined the whole world of people who wouldn't understand me through their brain or through their education, their statuses or their political positions, those to whom I wouldn't be able to prove the light, wisdom, or my experience. I saw their resistance. But I knew all I could do is to love. My love was huge, and it was not coming from me; it was coming *through* me. I imagined how I would just give them all love, because one day they will all know and feel it… *one day they all will, even if it's only for a moment, even if it only happens when they leave this world. But all of them will feel it, one day.* That is the TRUTH.

Tower of Light

6th Chakra

"Karma is always working."

"You are only who you truly are, not what you do for living or how society sees you."

"You can feel love when you believe in love, and that's what is healing for you."

"We can only be guided to take the next steps through trusting ourselves."

Chapter 7

Native American Indians

Tower of Light

Native American Indians

I was packing the whole art studio. A couple of friends were helping me. I had no idea what I would do or where I would go. Ever since my accident, I had been unable to focus on my art and hadn't sold any of it. I was calm and focused. I said "thank you" every day to the light and to the silhouette of the guardian spirit behind me.

I created a painting as a gift for one of the friends who helped me. While we were talking about a custom portrait of his grandma he told me about the company from which I was getting the metal supplies for my paintings. He mentioned that the owner was expanding his business. I called him. He came two days later. He was sent to me; I knew it by the way he was talking. I told him about my wish to have an art studio and to raise money for children. He told me that he would build me an art studio next to his company; that I don't need to worry. I saw his light. I knew he had faith—whatever religion he believed in, it didn't matter—I could see his faith, his business experience, and the light coming from his heart. I knew he would be one of my friends for a very long time.

Misa Art

I moved my art studio there and knew that one day I would build with him, along with others, something big, though at that time I couldn't tell what it would be. I just had the "feeling." My journey started from that day, and all of it felt like a game. I knew nothing in this world is an "accident" or "luck." I knew too much; I knew now about the nature of synchronicity, and spiritual "coincidences"—that they're not really coincidences, that everything happens for a reason.

I asked with all my heart, and the souls came to me, to help me. One of my clients, who is also a friend, called from Florida. She said that she had heard what happened, and wanted to purchase some of my art.

I had some money to hold me over now. I was thankful, so thankful, for all of those souls. I never complained. I never said that I couldn't do it, or that I was scared. All I kept saying was "thank you" for all I had.

For some people, it can be nothing, because they want more, but I felt like whatever I had was enough. I knew that what had happened to me was necessary in order for me to be thankful. I used to take my life for granted. I didn't really appreciate my gifts, including my gift of life. Now I had no place to live, I had no money—but to breathe air and to know my purpose in life was the biggest gift of all.

"This delivery is for you." The UPS guy was standing at my door and handed me an envelope. Behind me were stacks of boxes filled with all my stuff. Moving is supposed to be one of the most stressful things, but I usually felt immune to it. I had moved sixteen times, often between cities, countries, and even continents. I was a pro at packing. Yet this time was a little different, as I had no idea where I was heading.

"What is it?" I asked him. He looked at me and said to sign the envelope. "I don't know," he answered.

Tower of Light

I opened the envelope. Inside was a beautiful card and a check.

"Dear Misa, this is not a loan. This is my gift to you, for you to buy a new computer. Please don't give up. You need to learn how to receive and not only to give. I love you."

The check was for the same amount as my lost computer, and the handwritten card was signed by my friend Kath. She had bought some of my art a couple of years before, and we had become friends. I started crying. I never in my life knew how to receive things, because I was always scared that my obligations afterwards would be greater. I knew only how to give. I gave art to fundraise money for kids; I gave art to people who I knew needed it. I gave all I could to those with pain, because I used to be in pain. Giving gave me satisfaction, but receiving? Sometimes my dad, when I was little, would give me something—and then, by yelling at me and beating me up, he would take it back.

When people experience such forms of abuse as a child, they don't know how to react to human kindness. I didn't know how to react to such generosity from my friend who sent the check—I just cried. I cried tremendous tears, and started to believe in human kindness—not only the kindness of the light above me, but the kindness of human beings, too. I knew in that moment that Kath was my King from a past life.

Misa Art

I was a warrior in my visions, those visions I had when I met my shaman for the first time—during that "ghost party," as I called it. I saw again how I used to protect her, as her warrior. She was my King and always cared about how I would help this world; I knew that in my heart. *She will do the same for me in this life.* I understood that we all have souls we meet again and again—and all of it is for good. Even the bad is there for a reason, and is good because it shows us goodness. The *karma* will change into *dharma*, your spiritual purpose in life. Human kindness exists in many forms. I put the envelope in my pocket and went to buy a new computer, so I could get to work on my web designs and emails.

I looked back over my shoulder. The silhouette of my guardian angel was still there. I felt how he smiled while I was leaving that night. I wanted to know more about how thankful and grateful we, as humans, should be. The art studio was set, but still I didn't have a place to call home. I didn't know where I would live—but I had the light with me.

"Learn how to receive, Misa—and trust in human kindness," I whispered into the air.

The Ceremony: December 22, 2012

December 22, 2012. It was supposed to be the end of the world. I was seeing all kinds of posts from people on social media making fun of it. Something inside me said, *don't make fun of things you don't know too much about.* It was almost exactly two months since my accident, and just a couple of days before I was supposed to drive with Tom the Shaman and his writer-friends to a Native American Indian reservation in South Dakota.

Tower of Light

I was reborn, and I wasn't making fun of it. I felt something totally different. I was quiet to my friends and the world of Facebook and social media. I felt that it was not the end of who I was, but the beginning of a new type of energy. I could sense it. My body was just vibrating differently that night. I was kind of *excited*, and didn't know why.

I didn't read into it much—but I started doing things differently, too. I was listening to myself, observing myself, and doing what the light in my heart was saying. My shaman friend Tom sent me an email about this "ceremony," so I went. I had no idea what this so-called "ceremony" was all going to be about, but I came with respect for whatever these people did or believed. I was a hungry observer with a new heart, like a sponge that craves water; only I was craving new experiences.

We formed a circle in someone's house in the Chicago suburbs. There were fifteen people in total. Tom had lots of different types of little statues and stones laid out in front of him. My soul dad, shaman, medicine man, chiropractor; he was all that in one. I remembered how he had laid me down on the massage table and sang to the spirits for me.

The "story time" began—music, songs, and prayers—much like when we were in the sweat lodge, only this time we were on someone's floor. When it was my turn to say something, it felt natural to speak in front of the circle, not like the first time in the sweat lodge when I had been scared about what to say. I knew that whatever I said would be just fine, because I felt in my heart that I really meant it. I lost the fear of being judged by society. I was free. So, calmly, I spoke:

"I wish that of all of what was given to me, I will be able to give back. I wish to learn how to receive love naturally, because we all have gifts and those gifts were given to us so that we can give them away to others. I wish with all my heart that the suffering in me will find peace, and I wish the same for each of us. I would like to learn how to forgive fully, without words. I would like to say that I am so thankful to be here and feel the ground and see the light and faith. I would like to help children. Please give me more strength to be able to do what I was sent here to do."

I didn't wish to meet my soulmate or find love. I knew it wasn't the time to love only one person, but to love many. I wanted to love differently, not in the "normal" relationship sense. It wasn't that I didn't feel lonely sometimes while I was healing from my accident, or that I had no partner to hug me; but the light told me something else. I knew that for that time, I would not love intimately, but rather to share my light and love with many souls—and first, to love myself. My heart changed, and the horrible memories of my childhood were like a book, far away and impersonal. I felt that I was taking baby steps into this new world of LOVE and LIGHT.

After the ceremony, we had food at the house. My eyes were wide and my pupils were huge, like I had taken drugs or was on an LSD trip. My heart was beating fast, and I was so happy that I just smiled, joked, and laughed and laughed—but when I tried to look around, behind me, or in my peripheral vision, I couldn't see "him"—I came closer to my shaman friend and waited to speak to him. He was talking to other people. I needed to ask...

Tower of Light

"Tom, Tom... Tom... Do you see him? Do you see him?" I was in a panic—my guardian silhouette had disappeared. I couldn't see him, or feel him. Ever since the accident he had always been there.

"No," Tom replied, and continued talking to other people.

I didn't stop. "Where is he?" I was a bit upset, like a child who lost their imaginary friend. I couldn't tell anyone, but to Tom I could say anything. For example, "Last night this ghost dude came to me and said, 'Hey, can you stop snoring?'"—in Tom's and my world, that was a totally "normal" thing.

He finally turned away from the other people and came closer.

"Wow, you are glowing, look at your eyes," he smiled and looked at me more closely. "He is ...."

"Where *IS HE*?" I almost screamed. My shaman friend wasn't replying fast enough. Patience wasn't my best quality at that time.

"*Pssst*, HERE!" Tom pointed to my heart. "He is in your heart."

I was quiet; I couldn't understand.

"He *is* you... he was *always* you. Now, he is inside your heart."

I touched my heart instantly, like I was scared to lose it, and I felt love. I didn't understand the spirits, or the light in my brain, or the logic behind any of it. I had no experience or instructions to follow—*what do you do when your guardian angel, or "other half" or whatever, is inside your heart? Do you do this, do that?...nah.* I had no idea. Logic can take you from point A to point B, but creativity can take you anywhere.

"Your third eye opened when you were four years old, then it grew all over your face. You couldn't understand the amount of information, but now it is where it should be. And you have the switch, too, after the accident. You can radiate light, move in the visions, and feel everything with LOVE." He smiled and whispered, "Beautiful."

I was standing there, frozen. I could feel the love in my heart. I left everyone in that house without saying goodbye. I never like to say goodbye, ever. That doesn't exist for me. The poet Rumi says, "Goodbyes are only for those who love with their eyes. Because for those who love with heart and soul, there is no such thing as separation." I started to walk home alone, with my palm on my heart. "Nothing and no one or anything, they don't disappear. It is all here. I don't understand it, I just FEEL IT—I LOVE YOU, I LOVE YOU UNCONDITIONALLY, I love you while I love me... so this is SELF-LOVE? YES! I LOVE you, I love to know that you don't have white wings, you have grey wings with dark tips. And you LOVE ME UNCONDITIONALLY, too.." I wished for all people to feel self-love. Many people will misunderstand the meaning: it is self-love, but not selfish. It's not love for the ego-self, but the love of the true self, that it, naturally has for itself because our true self *is* love.

Tears were running from my eyes, and the moon was so bright... I knew I was no angel, even though angels followed me everywhere now. I knew that I made lots of mistakes in my life, but they were not mistakes... they happened for a reason, and I LOVED MYSELF now—unconditionally—like I loved that other part of me, the part who had protected me and stood behind me since the accident. We all have those, and they love us unconditionally.

Tower of Light

That night was supposed to be the end of the world, but for me, it was the realization of self-love, and it merged with my awareness of the whole world, shining like a little stream of light through my heart and outward in all directions. *If you love yourself then you can love others.*

I felt loved, both by myself and by the light from my guardian in my heart. At that time I had no idea how much I didn't know about all of these "LOVE THINGS" and who I fully AM. Life is a mystery, even for people with their third eye opened—especially when they are two months old. I was like a child in the body of a thirty-three year-old blond girl who used to love partying. I kept my slowly-growing world of LOVE a secret, and continued in the art business. I had to for my own survival; I needed to have a ground to stand on. But I knew I had to be like an actor, that I could only share this information with those humans who had a similar light around them. There are plenty of spiritual people who belong to various religions and beliefs, but I didn't care about that. I cared only about the light. I saw the levels of consciousness in everyone and became a chameleon with no judgment, who saw only LOVE. I slept very well that night and had a dream about deer with beautiful eyes running into the woods. I knew one of them was me.

Heart In My Palm

"Look at the sky, the eagle!" My Urban-Shaman (which is what I started calling Tom) was sitting in the passenger seat, and his friend Dan was driving. He was pointing out the window of the old Chevrolet car far away in the distance, to a huge bird flying in the sky.

Misa Art

"Look at the sky!" They both were looking at the sky with loving eyes, and I was scared that, while enjoying that big bird, he would forget to drive straight on the highway. I was sitting in the back seat and laughing at how these two older guys were having some major "bromance," with their mutual understanding of their own world and their friendship, spirits, and nature. It was beautiful to see. I was thinking of the connection I share with some of my friends, Gina or Jana (my friend from the Czech Republic). Those connections are just so natural, those people feel like your family. To understand that they really were family in your past life illuminates our understanding of who we are and who we will become later in life. Those soul-connections are here for us in this life and beyond, even when we leave our body.

I had three weeks to move out of my place, still not knowing where to, but when they invited me to join them and two young writers to meet a Native American Shaman of South Dakota named Ed, I just knew that I had to go. I wanted to feel *more*; because of the light I was hungry for the traditional native stories, for life, for everything; a new excitement was blooming within me; I was still holding LOVE in my heart. Every day, whenever something happened, I noticed that I was reacting to people and situations differently. I just closed my eyes and imagined the light again, and thought of my guardian protector. All of my problems felt small. All the things we have to face in life felt small.

Tower of Light

After eleven hours of driving, we stopped by a little road where, seemingly in the middle of nowhere, a huge man was standing. We pulled over, parked our two cars, and walked to him. It was the real-deal Native American Shaman, Ed. He didn't talk. He only moved slowly. I saw the worries and wisdom in his wrinkled face. Later, I made a sketch of that face, and gave it to him. He didn't know how beautiful he was. I realized that my perception of beauty had changed: before it was this shallow beauty; now I saw only the light, the *real* beauty. He was quiet for our whole visit. I felt his power, and I felt the power of the land where he took us. The trees were crooked from the energy of the Earth. His walk was always slow and strong. On the day he took us to the praying mountain, I felt a strong vibration in my legs.

My legs were vibrating more and more as we climbed the mountain. It was me, Dan, Tom, and two young girls who were writers. It was snowing closer to the top; Ed moved us closer to the wall of the mountain. I felt the mountain; I was vibrating and tingling as if ants were crawling all over my legs. I looked in panic at those girls—they were quiet.

Mr. Shaman in South Dakota, Ed, moved slowly in front of us. It was cold and snowing. He drew a circle in the snow and moved his hands into the open air and was holding his body in a position that looked like the tree pose in yoga. He started to mumble some words. It was snowing, and I saw an eagle fly over us and him. I didn't move, because no one was moving. I started to vibrate more, and my heart was pounding. From nowhere, I realized that snowflakes were not falling into my face anymore. I saw the back of his body standing there with arms to the sky. It stopped snowing, and a beam of light came through the sky and shined directly on him. It lasted two minutes. I looked at the girls next to me. Their eyes were like mine, full of surprise.

We all understood that something was happening, and it all happened within two minutes: the power of nature, respect, and prayer; the connection between human energies; and honoring the Earth. We all understood that this medicine man had just changed the weather in front of our eyes. We had witnessed a true channeling of human light and faith.

We all came down from the mountain, deeply quiet both inside and outside. It was then that my Urban-Shaman told me, while walking behind our huge Dakota-Shaman, who was again quiet, one piece of wisdom:

"You can feel the whole world's suffering. You can feel human pain. You do have compassion for those who suffer. Just remember, do not leave it all up to you. Leave it up to spirits, too." On that mountain I felt something; it was like the Hippocratic Oath that doctors have to sign, promising that no matter what happens they have to help humans. All shamans make the promise to the Earth and spirits that they cannot say no if you ask them for help. No matter who does the asking, they have to help; or at least begin journeying towards that.

Even the priests who existed in the past, the same ones who pushed and hurt Native American families, came to the Shaman Ed for help. He could never say no. No matter what they believed, no matter who they hurt, even their family—he had made the promise not to refuse them. He sees all humans as the same, with the same light, the same... and he is here to give love. I saw his heart, his green-aura; but I saw his suffering, too. It was a big responsibility to be a medicine man.

"Thank you," I said to the man standing with a huge body and with that big green heart. *The medicine man: Ed.*

Tower of Light

I knew I would use my gifts for good, but I was glad that I didn't make the promise of medicine men. On that mountain I learned how to say "no" with love, and simply give love and leave some things up to the spirits. "Some things you cannot change, so leave it up to the spirits," my shaman and friend's words would stay with me forever.

I learned how not to feel guilty if I just couldn't help or change the "weather." I understood the amount of my own light and faith on that praying mountain. When we were driving back home, we had to stop to let a whole family of deer cross the road, just like in the dream I had on the night of the ceremony.

One of the deer stopped and looked at me. His eyes reminded me of the little boy in my nightmares before the accident. Finally, slowly, I started to understand the unbelievable connections of all of these things, the signs and other stuff that was in the light coming from above while I was on the street. Since that day I started to google animal meanings and every animal I met, bird or bug—especially when they appeared unexpectedly. I started to realize that everyone has those "callings."

They are talking to us non-stop. We are the ones who are not listening. Mine were birds… birds were always the ones to bring me messages. Because somehow, all of the animal spirits are telling us something…

The next morning we had to say goodbye to Ed the Shaman, after a night in the sweat lodge. He was quiet, like always, sitting in his chair. This was the first time I could really hear his voice in full. He looked at me.

Misa Art

"You. What do you have in your hands?" I panicked, first of all because he was speaking to me, and second of all because I had no idea what to say—my hands were empty.

"I have everything in my hands, I am an artist, so whatever I feel, I do with my hands." I replied with a shaky voice.

"Close them now, and come closer," he said from his old chair in the corner.

"Please be careful with me, I am very sensitive, Mr. Shaman South Dakota." I felt a huge respect towards him—with a bit of fear, but mostly enormous curiosity. I closed my hands and moved closer to his chair.

"Ok, now open your left hand, the one from your heart," he said calmly.

I was standing in front of him and could feel his strong, calm energy.

I opened my palm slowly, like I was afraid of my own hand.

"Wow," I whispered. I felt my tears again running from my cheeks—tears of joy.

There it was, a small heart made out of ashes. It was as if someone had painted it in the palm of my hand. *Magic!* He started giggling... that huge old man started giggling, and with him my friend Shaman Tom, like I was their child.

"Love, I have in my hands, Love!" I whispered, and my eyes got wide.

It was the first time I saw Ed smile.

Tower of Light

It was the first and last time, because the beautiful Shaman Ed died a year after our visit. He decided to go, I knew he just decided to go, and to leave his wisdom here. He felt much of the world's suffering, and he helped all he could. He knew that, too. He sat in that same chair, closed his eyes, and just left his body—a year later. He gave me so many gifts, but the most important thing was that he reminded me that I have that heart of "his" in my hands already.

I still can feel his energy sometimes, mostly when I am in a place where people have hope: churches, temples, and spiritual events. I always look at my palm and a little, light silhouette of that heart appears as a shadow, and I think of his wisdom and love. I felt that powerful heart when one of my friends had a problem with his baby. The baby couldn't poop since he was born. I knew I had something in my hands. I came and touched the baby. "In five minutes, he will poop." Everyone stopped laughing when it happened.

I use it only in cases of babies or people who truly need my "hand." Sometimes I would touch a woman's stomach and pray for her to get pregnant when she can not; later it would happen. I know the power of love is in my hands. It's magic. It is LOVE. Later, when I was tattooing people I knew, I channeled my love from my heart through my hands as well. I decided to tattoo only spiritual things. I knew I would only tattoo those who were sent to me—not for a business, but for a reason—those who I can share that light with forever; same as my art, same as my heart.

7th Chakra

"To believe in human kindness is not a weakness. It shows the strength of vulnerability."

"The art of giving is equally important as the art of receiving. Love is a flow."

"The more love you feel for yourself and inside yourself, the more love you can give others. Everyone has angels."

"Find your gifts, then give them to the world."

Chapter 8

King and Priest

Tower of Light

King and Priest

I realized when I got home that I had only three more weeks to stay in my apartment, and then I would have to leave. To pay for my art studio and my apartment while I was still not physically able to sell art or paint or make money—it was just not happening.

I was doing my own physical therapy, yoga, every day. I knew I probably wouldn't be able to stand on my head like I used to; I knew there would be things I would never be able to do. I used to speed downhill on a snowboard as fast as I possibly could—that vision was put aside. But, for the first time, I was patient with my own body. I remembered those kids with cerebral palsy and especially one of them: Oly, whom I loved and love dearly. Some were in wheelchairs all their life, yet they were loving and appreciating life. *Who am I, here, to complain about a little memory loss and a poor sense of direction?*

My body was carrying light—*it needs it to be healthy, for I am the light.* I stopped eating red meat—not for any societal reasons, but because I observed that if I drank lots of water and ate lots of greens and less oils and fried things, then my visions got brighter. My intuition was working better. I started to listen to *me*, the inside of me. I started to walk without limping, and my vertigo became eased.

Misa Art

My blond hair, which would always grow thin when I was worried or depressed back in years past, started to get thicker. My face started to glow with this light, and people started asking what was different about me.

"Everything," I always replied. "Just everything."

We all are growing differently as we experience life, and that growth is measured by time and age here on this Earth. I knew I was getting younger-looking, but older inside. I was growing; but rather than taking years, it was happening day by day, very fast. I could sense books. I just looked at the book and knew what was inside, and knew if I should or read it or not. It was the same with people. I didn't judge them, I just knew who to "read" or not. If someone had weird energy or ghosts around them, I didn't run like I used to, afraid that their "ghosts" would jump on me. I stood my ground and was kind—even more kind to them. I listened to their problems, but their problems no longer entered me. I observed, helped, and let go. My heart was getting stronger, the light was growing. When my friend Kath called, I felt safe. And then, she saved me.

"Misa, just pack your stuff and store it at your art studio and come live with me for a while, while you get on your feet. I will help you. Through you, I will be able to help many, I just know. Can you come to church with me?"

Tower of Light

It was Kath on the phone, the same Kath who sent me a check for my computer after I was robbed. That same Kath I had seen in my vision as a kind priestess—as a king. She had great power in my past life, and she had power in this life. I knew I would bring back the light in her, as she would bring me love and support. The exchange of energies is important between humans. She was my King. I chopped some heads off for her as a warrior, I saw that, too. It was the time to change the karma. We were about as different as people can get. I was an artist with ADD. She was a very successful CEO-accountant with OCD, as well as a Catholic. Imagine the combo. And it worked. It worked because there was a purpose: love, unconditional acceptance, human kindness, and energy exchange.

I was always very independent and careful about people giving me things. I never wanted to feel obligated.

I never knew how to ask for help—and even more, I never knew how to receive it when I was in trouble. But I dressed up for church that Sunday. Not because I felt obligated, but because I felt like doing so.

"It is Father Tom today," said Kath, my King. She was sitting next to me in the church seats. It was Catholic church: beautiful, clean, and familiar. I had a strong feeling that I had been sitting there way, way back, long ago. It was stronger than déjà-vu. My soul was vibrating.

I looked up at the ceiling while they were singing songs, and around above the people in that church, I saw light. I saw the hope that they were all seeking. Everyone in the church had that floating light around them. I really liked it. I never would have expected to be sitting in that church because I wasn't Catholic—I had no religion—but I felt the need to be there.

Misa Art

My religion was LOVE and that LIGHT, which I didn't want to give a name to because I had so much respect for IT.

I wouldn't have been sitting there if it weren't for Father Tom, My King, and that floating light. I was pretty sure that during my accident, in that light, Jesus had been there, too. Because of the hope of all his followers, his light was quite large in the whole light of Wisdom.

The way we humans took the light into "our hands"—that was a different story. I noticed that Father Tom had that familiar green light in his heart, the same as the Native American shaman in South Dakota and my soul-dad-shaman, Tom. His heart was huge, filled with compassion for this world. He was *real*, and I knew that he had to follow the order of that church, but his light was pure and he had to go through so much suffering on his own to understand that. I understood that in order to have compassion for humans, you have to go through suffering; similar experiences are what make us understand each other on deeper levels. Only then is there a deeper understanding and compassion. I knew he was different, that priest—I knew it when he invited a female Jewish rabbi into the church, and let her sign in her name in the Catholic church. I knew it when he let gay people be helpers of the church. I saw his path for this world, and human hope. I saw his heart.

Father Tom had the light of hope and compassion, so I didn't care about his religion. I truly didn't care what people call it—he had the light. Sometimes I wanted to hug him and say, "It's ok… it will be all ok, because I know you are trying," because even trying is a beautiful human quality.

Tower of Light

When they all got up for communion, I was the only one in the church who remained sitting down until they received their communion, the "body" of Jesus. It was their ceremony and I respected it; but in the other ceremonies I went to, like the sweat lodge, no one asked if they could or could not pass the pipe or gesture toward the prayer-energy above them, because there everyone could act freely. In this church were rules—rules made up by humans, not the spirits. But I understood, too, that if you are not directly connected to the light, how can you know? How can you see the light if you can't see or truly listen to it through you? They didn't see the light yet, like I did, but they were hoping that it was there. All of these "church" people were following instructions, but I didn't judge them for it. They were trying, and that trying made sparks of hope burn in their hearts. I had hope for them. I longed to hug them with no judgment, only love.

"Hi Father Tom, may I?" I asked as I got up to try to receive communion.

I wasn't baptized. He looked at me with surprise and a heavy heart, and started to shake his head—"Please, no, you know you can't take communion."

Misa Art

I sat back down on the hard wooden bench. I knew he would love to help or give anything to anyone, but he was being held back. He was being held back by rules, by religion. Sometimes I think of how much I would love to take him out of that church and show him what he can actually do with that light of his, outside of church. But I saw his path of giving. I knew why I met this priest. I felt that later, understanding all of this would come to me. I felt I knew him from a past life, because Kath had brought me to him. That's the way it goes—if you feel a past life connection with a person, usually that person brings you to others who you were connected to before.

That day, Kath asked me to make a painting for him. She gave me money and asked me to give it to him as a gift. I painted my guardian; yet in the painting he saw Jesus. Whenever someone sees their light, faith, or any hope in paintings, it is their own truth—and I let them see whatever they see in it. Truth is hard to name. Truth has no name. Truth just is. Truth is hard to touch or to define. I had no need to prove anything or to name it, I just felt it. I had no rules for it. Though I had no name for it, I believed.

Kath had a Buddha in her home as well as a cross—and at the end of the evening, she had me, too. *My King and I, her warrior from a past life.*

I understood that in this life we are all growing alongside many souls from many past lives, and that if we all knew our past lives, it would be easier to move faster in this one. We are repeating our patterns, and we are here to learn from them or change them.

Tower of Light

The truth is here to help us understand our own behavior. It is easier to understand the truth of that light if you watch your own behavior—not the behavior of others, but first your own. You and only you are the truth of that light, which is connected to all.

Me and Kath were somehow connected. We both knew that we had met for a reason, and that the reason was coming nearer. She showed me how to receive and accept help. I felt it was my path, for now, to do just that. She showed me how to focus on the ground instead of always letting my head fly in the clouds.

I was praying with her in that church the same way I was making wishes in the woods. I was doing it every morning in her house. I was making wishes while I was holding hands with her and people around us.

I felt my little heart in my palm, but I knew it wasn't about the place where I was praying, meditating, or making wishes. I just liked different places, places where people had that hope, no matter where it was. They hoped for better things and to believe in good things. I didn't care about the restrictions of their religion; they all were a piece of that light for me.

Misa Art

After church I went to do kundalini yoga, meditated with gurus, and sang, and when I meditated there I could always see my guardian angel hugging me. He always came behind my closed eyes. I saw purple light and concentrated on it, and let all the outside world be. I liked that everyone was wearing white there. White started to be my favorite color. It was supposed to bring higher consciousness. Its purpose was to celebrate the light. And because I felt the light, I started to wear white, too. Not because of the rules of kundalini yoga—only because when I wore the color white I just felt lighter, more pure. I did it all because I *felt* it.

I was meditating because I could always feel him there—the guardian who was me, around me, and in me, just like my grandma, just like that white light. I had a church inside me, like all of us do, and through that purple light behind my closed eyes, my intuition was guiding me higher. I saw children, I saw myself floating above many children. When I told that to Kath, she helped me to open a charity for children. I painted with children who needed help, children with cerebral palsy, children from poor families—I painted with them and taught them how to breathe, what energy is, what to do when we have nightmares, what to do when we are in love, what to do when we have heartaches, what do to when we are rejected, what to do when we are having fear... and then I raised money for them.

"Are you a human?" I once asked one very hyper little boy in my class. "No, I am just crazy," he replied. I smiled. *How clever he will be one day...*

Tower of Light

"Don't you worry, we all are crazy here." *There is a very tiny edge between crazy and genius*, I thought, and I hugged him tight. I was always smiling when I was around kids. Their light is so pure and untouched; their soul is so clean. Yet the way this society teaches them how to be successful humans... I couldn't understand, or agree with. I felt we should teach them how to listen to themselves—it's all in there, that piece of truth.

My friend who built my metal art studio next to his company became one of the members of my foundation. He became my knight; later on I found out that he was the knight of Malta. My other client and friend who called me after the accident to buy my art also became a member. The lady I had seen as my spirit mom and her husband, who was fighting cancer, both became my supporters. All the people who believed in me started to show me every day that they believed in me and my light. I was thankful. I was thankful for my King and for the power of human love. I was thankful that all I can do is heal; it was healing me at the same time as it was healing many others. I was sharing only what I knew, and when I felt it was too much, I simply left it up to the spirits. To all the spirits and the humans in many places I simply said:

"I am not here to follow, I have no need of followers; I only collect the leaders of LOVE. *Wahe guru*, amen, *namaste*, *na zdravi*, and all which celebrate LOVE and LIGHT."

I didn't read it anywhere. No one taught me that. I just FELT IT. And that was a small piece of my truth.

"You will go on a spiritual journey with your friend, the Jewish rabbi. And, I will invite you and her to a big celebration one day," I said to the Catholic priest, Father Tom, one Sunday at church.

"Who are you? Who is she?" He asked, turning his surprised face to Kath after church. "How does she know? She is right, I am leaving for Jerusalem with a female Jewish rabbi this summer," he said.

"I just feel it, I just feel the change and light for many," I said, and gave him a hug.

I felt a warm feeling and change for this whole planet. I felt a white light of hope and peace in that moment of hugging him. My soul knew that I hugged him many many lives before 2. I felt that his rabbi friend walked with him before too in a past life. I wished that this time they would fulfill the purpose of why they met. I wished that they would see their truth.

Tower of Light

"Love and light see no religion; they both are just pieces of simple faith."

"If your purpose is for many, you will always find your "king" to help you or to move you closer to your truth."

"There is light beyond anything that we can see with our eyes; everyone sees this light in proportion to how deep they see into the Spirit world."

Chapter 9
Amma

Amma

My Shaman Tom called. "Amma is coming to the USA, and she is going to allow me to bring Native Americans into her traditional Indian ceremony. Will you go with me?" I knew I would invite my King Kath as well.

At that time I had no idea who Amma was. I googled her name and found out that she is an East Indian mother, something like a Mother Teresa. Her story was beautiful, and her faith was love. She was their "hugging saint"—in fact, she was the world's hugging saint. She started to hug people in India when she was a little girl.

No one understood why this little girl, who grew up in India, believed that hugging people was what she needed to do. It was new; especially since women are generally not allowed to touch anyone, especially if you belong to a certain caste. She was born to give love to people with her hug. There was something in her—she had it in her. She was an Indian goddess who opened one of the biggest humanitarian organizations for people and children in her later years. Now she was a fifty-year-old Goddess of Goodness, who traveled and had many ashrams all over the world.

I channeled her and could feel from miles away that she was powerful, but I had no idea what I would experience later. She was open for love and her secret hugging. She hugged millions and millions of people. I knew I would love to be hugged by her and to feel her energy. They said that whatever you need, you will find in her hug. I invited Kath and Tom, and I started to drive to Amma's ashram a couple of hours outside of Chicago.

While we were in the car, I saw a homeless person by the road. He asked for money. I was usually a very generous person, but I didn't give him money. From her seat in the passenger seat, Kath asked, "Misa, why didn't you give him any money when he asked?"

"I have a gift to see what he will do with that money. He will get drunk and hurt many," I answered, calmly driving my car.

"But we should give without judgment," she replied, in her generous—maybe Catholic—way.

"Without any judgment, I say this: that you are right. But I could see what he was going to do with that money because I'm psychic, and he wasn't thankful." I replied. After thirty minutes of driving, I stopped and gave change to another homeless person.

"To this one I will give. He really needs it; he is not making the whole world responsible for his life. He is not a victim of his situation."

My shaman friend smiled. He was watching us the whole time from the back seat, and listening to our conversation. "Just like Amma," he said, and started to share a story with us. I smiled at him in the rear view mirror.

Tower of Light

"Amma hugged hundreds and hundreds of people every day. But one day a blind woman came to her and waited for her hug, and Amma didn't pay any attention to her." I smiled at him again. I knew there was always something in his stories.

"Why don't you hug me, when you hug millions of people?" the blind woman asked Amma.

Amma didn't reply and left the blind woman standing there, without her loving hug. A year later the blind woman came to Amma again, and Amma hugged her with so much love.

"Why did you not hug me before, last time, when I asked you to? I waited for your hug over a year," the blind woman asked.

"Because you were blaming the whole world for your situation. Because you were more blind than you think. Now you are not playing the victim of what happened to you. Without the hug you were angry; you needed that anger to learn. I gave something to you without giving it to you."

The blind woman cried and thanked Amma for her hug.

When my friend shaman finished the story, I knew... *I really want to meet this Amma, this hugging saint. She is kind, real, and true.* We were five minutes away from her ashram, and I saw lines of hundreds of people outside, all waiting for her hug. It was like a palace, where everyone was waiting for their queen to give them something untouchable.

When I walked in, Kath and her friend, who we met there, started to stand in the line. Amma, a small Indian woman wearing white rope, began her ceremony with a huge smile. There were hundreds of people. She was on the stage. Many people were chanting in front—but I couldn't enter the building. Her energy was very strong. The whole building was full of incredibly intense energy, because she was rooting her energy from the entrance.

As soon I walked in it was moving me. I started to be nauseous. Tom saw my face. He was so excited to come inside to say hello to her. He became a friend of the whole ashram later and built a Native American sweat lodge on her land. He had to leave me there. So I sat in front of the building on that chair and started to breathe, waiting for the moment when she would start hugging people. I saw from far away a light coming not from her to people, but from above her and down through her. I wasn't sure, at that moment, if she was human. There was not a bit of fear in it, no suffering—only pure LOVE. She was the first person like that I had seen since the accident. It was something closer to that light. *Not a human... she is using the source straight from above.* I saw the whole place and the people having huge pupils in their eyes. This woman had a gift that was not coming *from* her, but *through* her.

She knew. After a while, when I heard that the opening ceremony had finished, and she was starting to hug people, I slowly walked in. I found my friend Kath and her friend in line.

"Hey, where were you? Are you ok?" they asked. "I was just resting." My eyes were looking at that woman—Amma, which means mother—on the stage instead of my friends. She was a tiny, smiling thing; she had a loving light coming through her. I was slowly moving through the line, closer to her. The energy calmed down. I felt people's hope.

Tower of Light

"So, now she will hug me and I will shit my pants?" I made that joke, not knowing that I was close to the truth! My shaman friend was running around and smiling at people; he was so happy, his pupils got wider, too. I couldn't stop staring at the stage. I could feel her.

"Where are you from?" asked one of the people on the stage while they were moving me closer to her. Everything was automatic. "Czech. Czech Republic." They moved me like a puppet toward her. It was fast. She was there, sitting on the throne. I was in her arms. She hugged me. I felt the light—not her light, but the light of the Highest Spirit, which I remembered feeling on that street, just for a second, when my body was hit by a car. I closed my eyes, and Amma whispered in my native language, "Babichka"—*grandma*—and I could feel my grandma hugging me. I felt her, even though she had passed away three years earlier. She was hugging me through her. I had tears in my eyes and I was weak, like a puppet. The people around me moved me away. I was in her hug for probably two minutes.

"You," the lady next to Amma said, "you need to sit here." She moved me onto the stage next to Amma and a couple of other people. I felt as if I had a huge balloon head, and I had no idea how to deflate it. This lady knew, like all of the people around, that I needed to sit down. I couldn't walk after the hug. I was sick. I felt so weak, but happy. I sat there for about half an hour, and my senses came back. I started to smile with a whole different energy in me. My friends, Kath and others, left, but I stayed in that ashram for twenty-four hours with my Shaman friend.

I didn't eat too much there, and I didn't sleep. I just didn't need it—I was charged up. I just wanted to stay in that place where she was hugging those little tiny ants, the people. *The chocolate smiling queen.* She was giving that light for three days, and she needed to sleep only three hours. I knew why. I saw Love, and I took that with me, in my heart, back home.

"Amma? Nah, she is not a human... she is a pure channel of that light," I said to my friends later. After I got home, I was sick for three days. I understood that I was detoxing. She just moved it—she moved something in me. It didn't heal me, something different was happening. That light just touches you in the core of your soul; it's for you to get from it what you need.

Maybe it was my sadness for my grandma, maybe that something that was still deep inside me. Maybe it was that I had no chance to tell her what her son, my Dad, did to us, because it was her son... *oh, Grandma.* And in that hug I could feel that she knew now, now that she was in spirit, and she wanted to tell me she is really sorry. That she is sorry and she loves me and she will be my help forever.

Tower of Light

Maybe I was still sad or I was missing her, but I understood that everything needed to come out of my body. The sickness was just detoxing. When we are sick, it is actually something which is stuck in us and it is leaving our body. It just needs to go, to leave. So I let it. We all should let go. I also started to understand that if we truly let go of many things, there will be a pain at the beginning, when you get so close to it in order to touch it, but after that is just release and peace. It always comes, you just need to believe that you are releasing and that every pain is temporary. I promised myself that any time I feel any sorrow, that I would remember that: to let go, to cry, to puke… anything. Because I am now in the hands of Spirits, which are my own hands, at the deepest level of my heart—which is Love.

Sometimes we don't even know that it's there, but then something "touches" us—music, humans, art, places, or even a Goddess like Amma—that helps us to move through things energetically. And it always happens so that we can let go. I will always remember that: TO LET GO. That was what Amma gave me. Not to be a victim of any life situations or of pain. To give, sometimes without giving. Just to let it in, feel it, and let it go.

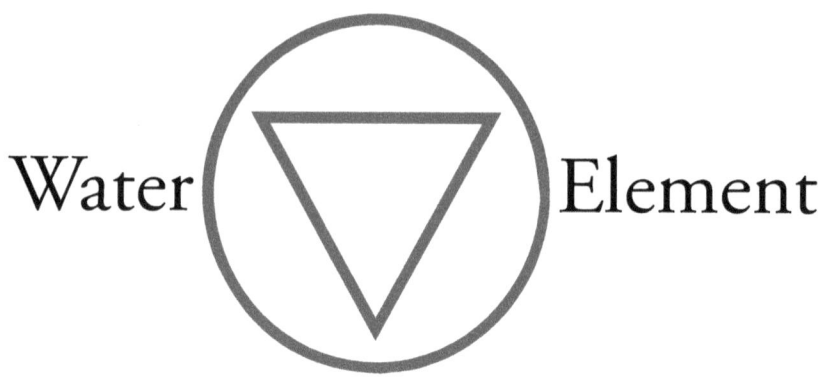

"Sometimes you have to touch the pain to let it go."

"Helping sometimes happens without giving, but rather simply by being."

"Do not ever be a victim of your life."

"There are big-beings who are pure channels for universal energy."

Chapter 10

Tarot Reader, Eagles and Pigeon

Tower of Light

Tarot Reader, Eagles and Pigeons

After a couple days of detoxing, painting, and working with children, I was in my new studio painting and getting ready for an upcoming show. I was enjoying the solitude. I didn't feel the need to drink or party. I didn't feel lonely. I was just happy to be left alone. I didn't hear weird noises or see ghosts or have any predictions. I felt the ground, and I felt like a normal person. Well, obviously not fully "normal" after the head injury and crazy out-of-body experiences—but my hair grew back and I could start running again and doing yoga fully. I felt simple. I tried to make my life simple as it could be. I felt happy. I felt like a human.

Misa Art

"Hello, knock, knock!" Someone was knocking at the door of my art studio. *Grr, now when I don't feel like moving an inch, someone is here. I think that my alone time is for everyone's safety.* I had to smile to myself at that joke, and opened the door. Some lady was standing there holding a jar of honey. She was asking about the metal company next door. But as soon she saw me, she just wanted to come in and see my art. I had become a bit of a public person as an artist, but was still holding my private life and my visions to myself. *What is "normal" in this life anyway? We all are equally crazy, some of us just know that we are and accept ourselves. Those are the truly happy crazy people.* She was looking at me strangely, as if I was "crazy"—which I was, in a way—but not in the way that she might have thought.

But I let her in. I felt that there was a reason why she missed the other door and came to mine. I knew that, even with people on the street, strangers, there was some reason to get lost for them to find me. We get lost only to be found, or to find something. Somehow she found me, so I let her in.

She sat on my green sofa. She was quiet for a bit and still holding that jar of honey. I could start feeling her sorrow. I knew what was coming.

"You know my son, my son was an artist... he fell from a roof and died. We don't know what happened that night in NYC, but he was smoking a cigarette on the roof of his apartment, and then they found him on the street, dead."

Tower of Light

I knew why she was here. I could feel it. The blurry silhouette next to her—she needed to let it go. I told her my story, the story of the light and hope. I tried to explain it on her level of consciousness, so that she could understand. But her heart was closed from the pain. *For now that's it, I thought, that is all that I can share with her; because that's all she is ready for at this time.*

"But you came back, you came back and he didn't, he is gone." She was a bit angry, but mostly she was saying this because no matter how much I tried to explain it to her, she refused to accept it. She kept saying, "I don't know, it was an accident."

I couldn't tell her that he was around, that his light was here forever. I couldn't explain to her that nothing is an "accident" in this world. I couldn't tell her that she gave the body to him, but that no one owns the light; the light was given to him, and only him, to go back to the Spirit world. I wasn't a mother who had lost a child, so my level of compassion couldn't satisfy her. I couldn't explain to her that everything always happens for a reason, for us to learn—even through the loss of a loved one. So I left it up to the spirits and to the one next to her. *There is a time for her to heal, there is a time for her to understand why her only child died.* She was angry at the whole world. She was hurt.

Misa Art

I knew that anger was a part of her steps toward healing. I knew that the opposite of love is not a hate; I knew the opposite of love is our fear. She had that fear of the unknown, like many of us. She ended up here, on my sofa. I was thinking about how many people had sat right there, on that sofa, and cried their eyes out. Some were here as my lovers, but that wasn't why she was here. Somehow the energy and experience of my light called her. My only mission here was to listen to her and say nothing. She felt close to the art, because her only son had been an artist. I gave her the comfort of that, and just listened.

"All I can tell you is that it's beautiful there," I said while I hugged her after she had given me that jar of honey. I added, "He didn't commit suicide, if that was your question."

She smiled in surprise and I closed the door behind her. I hoped that I closed the door of her guilt too. She felt somehow guilty that she wasn't able to stop it, that she couldn't save his life. *We can't, we are only humans.* So I gave her a print of my art called *Piece-full Forgiveness*, part of a four-painting series. She needed it to forgive herself. I didn't tell her that the first part of that series was a painting called *Denial*. *Nobody is responsible for anyone else's life, even for their own child's.*

I made myself a ginger tea with that homemade honey, and something came to my mind. *Questions.* I dialed a number that I had been carrying with me for a couple months.

Tower of Light

"Hello, are you open? Can I come? Today? Ok, I will be right there." I drove a couple miles from my studio and opened a glass door. I knew lots of people with different gifts. Gifts to see, to feel, to read the past or future—there are many. Actually we all have those gifts, but some of us open to them more fully. Usually those who open a lot have had a near-death experience, or were close to their own death; mostly they can see many things, and can understand the "information" (spirit-world information) that comes through open channels of our soul.

In the room were shamans, psychics, astrologists, and other people who went through experiences like hard illness or accidents. I definitely could tell which ones were more open than others. I respected all people's gifts and talents; but with all gifts you have to be careful, especially when you are working with spirits and people's spirits. You have to be careful with your words. Words are very powerful. Anything you say has magic, the same as thoughts have. But because many people operate on Earth with words, you have to be careful "how you say it." Maybe that's why all of the shamans are always so freaking quiet, just like I was with that honey-giving woman at my studio. You have to be careful, especially when you are psychic. This one was one of them. I sat across from her. I knew that there are paths in life, with many options to get there, but usually everything comes full circle in life, no matter how much of a resistance you have, or what you think you know or can control. We have no control. What we can do is ask if it resonates with our path or melody and it will come, always. That's what I learned from that light "above."

I checked her out again, and her energy. I was pretty close to being in her aura space. "Aura space" is the space around your body. When you spread your arms and touch the air, that's usually your aura bubble. She was very grounded and serious.

"Shuffle," she said. Then she looked at me and said, "you had an accident? I can see the right side of your body is weaker than the other." She "scanned" me in a psychic way, before she spread the cards. I smiled. *Well, this one gets it*, I thought.

She put the tarot cards down and I was calm. She looked at the cards, then looked at me. She knew that I knew. I scanned her as she had scanned me. It was actually funny to feel it. It felt like visiting an old friend, someone I knew; only that she wasn't my friend, she was a tarot reader. I felt curiosity for what she might see.

She picked up the card of death and looked at me. "This, this… you have a very strong angel. Actually you have many, but this one… You were not supposed to be here. The death card. Reborn. You came back. What happened?" I smiled.

 "Yep, I am back on this Earth to do crazy things," I joked.

"Well, not that crazy… I see… Can I ask you something?" she stopped looking at my tarot cards. "Did you see him? Or the light?" I smiled again.

"Yes, not his full face, but mostly his body and wings. How about you?" I asked her, and our positions of telling me my future changed.

"I felt him, I was there, just like you." She was older than me, and calm. She knew about her gift more than me, but I wasn't here to compete with anyone. I just hoped we would all "make it."

"It was a car, hit and run," I said.

"Well, they didn't catch the person who hit you, right? You lost all of your money and work, but if this had not happened, you would have been in jail for three years. This thing gave you more than anything, this brought you peace, this brought you a purpose to be aligned with."

"I would have killed a little boy with eyes like a deer, that night. If I wasn't hit by a car I would have killed him," I answered, and remembered the nightmares three weeks before the accident. I realized right there, *That's why I came to her, and saw patterns on situations and reasons and life, and I saw the lady with the jar of honey and her son… Someone or something didn't stop him. It was his time. But maybe his death stopped something else… oh, the meaning of those waves, of that light!*

"Probably, something like that," she answered, and looked down.

"You were sent here to bring… bring light… for people… light… or something… This wasn't your time. You are an artist and you are helping children. You lost the fear of society's judgment, you lost your fear of rejection, you lost your fear of being alone—you lost the fear of death, too, and one day you will be famous."

"We are never alone. So I have to work more? Hahaha. Nah, I don't want to be famous, famous people are usually very lonely. This world needs more healers than famous people. I just want to do what I love to do," I winked at her.

She continued to tell me a couple things that I already knew, but it felt comfortable to listen to someone who just had that gift and was "there." She was "there" and she wanted to help people with her gifts. I knew she couldn't tell them everything... there are things a tarot reader can't say. They are things you can't say to humans, or you need to learn how. It would change the whole life path of the individual. Always let people breathe, breathe their own space of the future; they will figure it out on their own time. I respected her gift. Maybe I just didn't want to have the responsibility for people's future to be formed by words. It wasn't my path to help them that way. My way was more with paintings and creations, that was my path—and maybe to forgive, forget, and start to have a bit of a grounded life for myself.

"Hmmmm... you are special, you need someone special for you." That's what she said at the end of her channeling speech.

"Don't we all?" I winked at her again. I knew that was true. I thanked her and when I was leaving the place of the "future" and "past," I saw on the wall a book she had written. It was a fairytale. On the cover was a painting of a woman and a man with big wings. He was strong, and was holding on to her with strength. I smiled again. *"Special," she said.*

To think about the future too much brings up anxiety and desires, what we think we need or want; to think of the past brings depressions. I knew both really well from previous lifetimes of non stop spinning and thinking. I wanted to stay in Present-Time, and to have that PEACE and LIGHT in my heart, simply to share. It wasn't anything I read in books or heard in yoga classes. It was my wish.

Tower of Light

I knew that was the best thing for me right at that moment. I knew I was the one who had the "switch," for me. We all have the "switch," we just need to find it. Those people whose switch is too open, they need to calm it down, sometimes. So I tapped on my forehead, where my third eye was, and said out loud like I was speaking to a person:

"So have a rest, Mr. Third-Eye, you need it, NOW."

"Are you ok?" asked someone on the sidewalk who saw me tapping on my forehead and talking out loud.

"No, not at all, but I like it. They call it 'special.' By the way, how are you?" I replied to that stranger, who started to smile. I continued walking to my car and realized that it was the same street where my accident had occurred. We always return to places, things, or relationships, if we didn't learn the lesson from it. I knew I needed it to see that street to remind me. So I listened and I touched the scar on the back of my head again and said, "Thank you. I will." You can talk to yourself. We always do. There is the mind-voice, the heart-voice… and the intuition-voice, which is the third eye. There are many "voices" in us. I needed to listen to the highest one, which was above them all. "Seven to heaven," I whispered and smiled.

Many months later I visited another very famous psychic woman. She had been a psychic for Michael Jackson and other celebrities. She suggested that I should give to myself first, and then to other people. "You are an eagle. You need to find an eagle and stop playing with pigeons." I laughed. But I stopped laughing when she said, "You will write a book. It will be a world's bestseller and you will build something beautiful for humanity. Be strong."

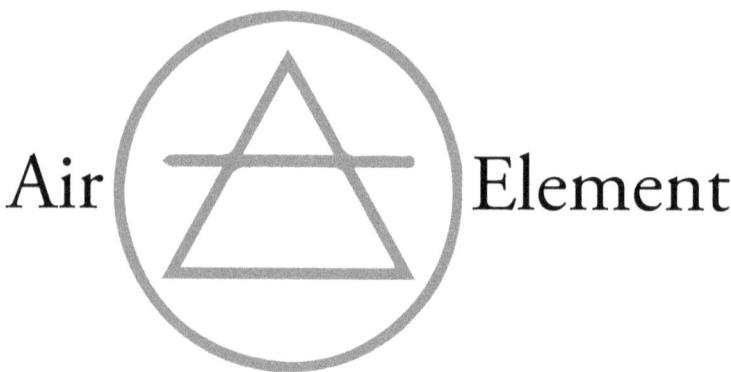

Air Element

"You are like a magnetic force to those souls who have similar experiences"

"Usually all relationships are karmaticlly based"

"When you get heartbroken, it is for you to learn, forgive and let go. The reasons will come with another seasons"

Chapter 11

Soulmates and Twin Flames

Tower of Light

Soulmates and Twin-Flames

After the tarot card reader mentioned something about a "special" guy, I started to take a deeper look at my life—in particular, my "love life." I could see clearly how many deep and real connections I had. The soul doesn't have male and female part. The soul is both. All of our connections with people are mostly based on karma. Karma can make something happen so that we can learn about ourselves through it. Sometimes it may appear that it ends badly (which is never bad); or sometimes we call it bad because it happened the way we didn't expect. We will all find out eventually, at the end, that all these things happen for good. To love with no expectations is hard, but it is the best way to love. To love with no ego is beautiful. The ego must die—only then is true love born.

"Some of them for a reason, some of them for a season, and some of them forever. That works for all of soul connections." That's what I used to say to my friend Jana in Czech, when we were young and crying about heartaches. The older you get, the harder it gets to get over relationships. Pilling the hurt baggage. But when you are more involved spiritually, you start to understand many things in different light—not only with "guys," but also with friends, family, and any souls.

When talking about love life, a lot of people talk about the idea of a "soulmate." Some people are lucky to stay with one soulmate as a partner. But soulmates are not only partners; soulmates can be just souls you knew from before.

Some people's soulmate relationships are a bit more complicated—it depends on the soul type, how old the soul is, or how much the soul needs to learn. I was over thirty-three years old, but had a new heart of a one-year-old and many past lives behind me. My ex-husband was my first soulmate, that I could clearly see. *What happened...?* Life happened, and I left after being hurt and betrayed. I was too young. But I knew that everything was just as it should be. The next partner represented what I thought I deserved after divorce. I didn't feel right about myself, so I attracted someone who would not be nice to me. I thought I deserved someone who will not love me. But again I learned, and left.

Then there are those "devil"-soul guys. Everyone meets this type of person at least once in their lives. Try not to marry them—bad idea. I chose, before this lifetime, to understand how my mom could be with someone so mean like my dad. I let him in my life to destroy my wings, and I started to believe that there was something wrong with me. He didn't break my heart—he just messed with my mind. I could see it now; but when I was in it, I was blind. Because of that, I was able to forgive my mom. I learned from it, too. I learned that I would never be with someone who didn't believe in my visions or dreams. People who try to put you down are simply people who don't like themselves. If you are weak, you will be addicted to their poison—it is our dark side. But I forgave him too.

Tower of Light

Finally after that, I met my second soulmate. *Green light.* The relationship was beautiful. You grow with soulmates. It goes in waves. You don't need to talk, they just know. There is always love and friendship. There is peace; and because I was a strong person, his kindness made me calm. There is always love, even when you are not together anymore. They take the position of your parent, sometimes your sibling, sometimes your child, sometimes your lover or friend; it changes. It is not only a sexual connection. Their faces change sometimes, too, as if you see many people in them.

I had to leave him too, but knew we will always be friends and there is love. He was the one who I wanted to see immediately after my accident.

And he felt me so much. We were so connected that once, when I was having vertigo after my accident, he fainted in front of my eyes with me!

Then there was the one who I painted; he was my muse. He was my soul brother in this life. I had no idea what was happening on many levels at that time, so I met my reflection again. We were never sexual. He was a female soul in male body. We come to this Earth with certain contracts with other souls. He just didn't sign the contract to be my partner. My soul remembered that we used to be together, but he just didn't "sign." As an artist, I was just happily obsessed with his beautiful, perfect body and his light. It was a muse/artist thing.

Misa Art

Since the accident I started to see more and more, and I could feel another soul fire coming. I just knew. I could have any guy I wanted, but I was tired of wasting my time on "empty" guys with no light. I was very busy with work and my foundation; but I wanted a soul fire, so I asked for it. Usually we don't get what we want, but what we need.

Once, when I was flying at night into Florida, I could see his light as I was leaving the parking lot. I could sense him. He was standing there, in the middle of the crowd—a bright, yellow-orange light. I saw his light and pain. I saw that fire. I saw that I was with him before. I also saw that he was not ready for me—that he was with someone else. I tried to move away from the crowd and run from the future, but someone stopped me. "Hi. I'm his father." The old guy smiled, and pointed to that standing light behind him. He was tall. He smiled and moved closer.

It was my soulmate. My light totally scared him.

"Who are you?" he asked, confused about why he could see me and the light around me. He was a financial guy in a suit, "seeing" me. We were both shaking. He knew me, I knew him—but we had just met. I saw a vision of him as my husband in a past life. I couldn't explain this to him. It would only scare him. "I see your light, you are glowing, are you a witch?" he asked, all confused. We danced; we felt it.

Tower of Light

Then he left. The connection was so strong that I could feel him every day, and every night. I saw him everywhere. He did too, and I knew it. But he was with someone and we didn't want to get hurt or hurt anyone. One year later, I met him again. It wasn't our time in this life to be together, but I still waited for him. I saw him in everyone. Yet he was scared of my light; he was not ready. He couldn't understand the power of love in me. But he felt my light. He couldn't logically explain anything about me. He loved me and he missed me, but he couldn't understand why. Our timing was just wrong. He knew; and he cried, too. He had the pain of his mother, as I had the pain of my father. It was our old pain connection, and we would carry it into our next life.

I accepted all of it with heartache; and I knew that in the same place, a year later, I would meet another soulmate who would love me, and who would give me a mirror-type wake-up call. I manifested him to move away from my visions of burning fire. I knew he would be in the same position as me. And I didn't feel ready. He hoped to forget about his pain through me. I hoped to forget about my pain through him. I knew he would be the one who would move my pain and make me laugh; that he would turn my pain into joy. I knew I would help him recover from his divorce, and help him to understand many things about himself. Love is a flow. I learned lots of things about myself when he broke my heart, too; and even for that, I thanked him. I sometimes saw my guardian holding him. If my angel liked someone, I knew it was the right thing at the time. When he broke my heart, I felt a force of pain—but even though for a split second I felt anger and disappointment for his own blindness, I tried to send only love.

Misa Art

It scared me that I was so angry. But it helped me remember that I am only human, and that I am entitled to feel angry too. I had to stop my guardian angel and my thoughts in order not to hurt him, because I knew our thoughts were powerful. We cannot wish anyone pain; otherwise it will come back to us. In seven days, in seven weeks, in seven months, or seven years, I had to leave. I could feel that he didn't want me to leave, but I couldn't stay, because to see my heart on the ground was hard and I didn't want to hurt anyone. I knew that I am LOVE. I knew that somehow I had hurt him before, in another life, which is why he hurt me now. That was my karma. Sometimes soulmates are here to break us into many pieces, so that we may finally see ourselves.

Sometimes they are not here to stay with us. In connections, time doesn't matter. A strong connection can last only a split second. Your soul just knows. Love is time, and time is divine. And there has to be forgiveness at the end, otherwise broken patterns will follow you into your next connections. Take your time to heal. If the time comes when you truly decide to change the pattern, lie down and imagine all of the connections with that person, and then start cutting the imaginary cords, like cutting the air above you.

That is the first step of disconnecting yourself from feeling them, no matter how they leave or how you leave them. Try to clear your space and believe that every pain is temporary. Believe that they are on their own journey, in which your role can only be to bless them with your good thoughts.

Tower of Light

It was like a theater play. I knew it had to happen and I had to be a part of it, no matter how much I didn't want to, no matter how much I could see. I knew I could not stop any of it, I only had to go through it. It had to happen. It was my karma and I accepted it; and learned from that love, and the pain too, just like when one of my boyfriends died when I was twenty years old and I knew it when I met him.

When you are an old soul you have many soulmates, but everyone has only one twin flame—the true other part of you. But my other part was at the astral level. That was my guardian. I knew that. After my third soulmate, I felt that the sparks would go down and I would be with a calm soul who would not be my twin flame, but who would be my "eagle" to help and support me.

I could feel his energy, but I knew I would have to wait. All of it happened, all of the heartaches and breakups, to help me focus on that light from the accident and to fulfill the purpose for which I was sent back. It was something bigger than being in a relationship right now. I knew my last partner would be someone who is already complete, who doesn't *need* my love. Love is not a need. I knew he would come one day when I would be fully complete myself, and not looking for healing or needing anything from anyone. *He will come when I am closer to my purpose. He will be ready and special.* I closed my eyes and smiled. I saw the number seven. *Seven years? Seven months... July? Seventh chakra?* I had no clue, but I saw the number seven.

"When will you have children? " When you will have a husband?" I could feel the social pressure of these questions. They couldn't understand that I just knew that now is my time of fulfilling my purpose and understanding my light.

So I said, "No more helping pigeons, only be with the eagle. He will come, I know. One day, when I will be ready myself… maybe at 7:00 a.m." I laughed and looked at my watch. Love is time, and Love is everywhere. I felt that piece of heaven coming in the near future.

Make that wish for yourself, but make sure you really know who you are right now at this moment, everything you are—and if you are complete. Those who you attract will be a reflection of you—for a reason, for a season, or forever.

"Sometimes one of the biggest proofs of love is to let go of our loved ones with peace. We as humans are in physical form, but our soul is eternal energy. We must let go with hopes to meet again."

"Words and thoughts are very powerful. Be careful with your words and thoughts."

"If love once existed, there will always be Love. If it is meant to be, it will be, whether in this life or the next."

"There are soul-mates that comes only for a certain amount of divine-timing;"

Chapter 12

Mamacocha

Mamacocha

We planned a trip to Peru. There is a saying that goes, "If you want to make God laugh, tell him your plans." Usually people go to Peru on vacation to see Machu Picchu, to hike, and take some photos. Well, this wasn't a vacation of that "style." It was truly the journey of my life, and the lives of those who went with us. I had a feeling that there was something I needed to see. I wasn't sure what, but that place had been calling me since I was six years old. I had dreams on a mountain and stairs, always I was always walking them up. It's good to follow your dreams, even if they are from childhood. When I saw Machu Picchu in pictures and heard that my shaman Tom was planning that trip, I knew—*I have to go, because IT is there, that is the place from my childhood dream.* I listened. It was in that dream, so I followed it.

I didn't know at that time that place would change my life and move me closer to understanding why I was touched by that light, and why I came back. It had been exactly one year since my accident, and I was a world traveler looking for that place. When someone said "Peru," I started to vibrate with very strong energies. I knew something was there.

Misa Art

My shaman Tom rounded together some people for the trip. No one knew each other previously. Emails were sent to fifteen people across the USA, with a recommended preparation diet and a brief description of the plan: eleven days of intense hiking in Machu Picchu and Amazonia. Every day we would be in a different place, and we would meet two Peruvian shamans. I invited my photographer friend, Mary Carol; a Polish filmmaker, Lukas; and Reena, a funny, young Indian girl with whom I opened a children's foundation earlier that year.

"What do they mean by no sex or alcohol five days before the trip?" Reena was reading the preparation for our trip. "Is the ayahuasca jealous? It's a plant that shamans drink at their ceremony, how can it be jealous?"

"You better behave and listen. It is a strong medicine that will show you things about yourself and the world, and other worlds," I said, while packing my hiking boots into my suitcase. I had gotten all my shots in a doctor's office for the insects in Amazonia. Yet I was starting to feel a bit nervous, because one night before the trip I had a nightmare. I hadn't had a vision of that type since before the accident. The spirits of Peru came to my bedroom. Two very tall, strong silhouettes were standing in the corner of my bedroom. I didn't move. In the morning, I had very strong vertigo and puked again. I hadn't puked for months since the head injury. I listened again. I listened to my body and the light in my heart.

"I will do the diet, but I have a strong feeling that I won't be able to do ayahuasca at the shaman's ceremony," I said to Reena and Mary Carol while we were walking out of the airport in Lima, Peru. The first thing I saw were the mountains. Then my feet started to vibrate. I felt Mother Earth right there. I felt a pressure in my ears.

Tower of Light

"Here, chew on that." Someone in the Lima Airport gave me coca leaves right at the door of the airport. "It is supposed to help with the altitude."

"Thank you... or the attitude?" I smiled and started to chew on the green leaves. It helped. I was chewing coca leaves and drinking coca tea. I felt energy; we all did. I looked at the group in front of the bus that would take us to Cusco.

We were thirteen people from the USA of various nationalities and aged from twenty up to sixty years old. Everyone had their own hidden story for why they came on this trip.

We all have our own story and questions. Sometimes we don't even know that we have those questions because they are so deep inside, because we buried them. But one question is the same: do we want to know? Or are we scared of the truth; the real, raw truth? Some people are not ready to see it, because the TRUTH is RAW.

But all of these people were here to get something from this journey. I was proud of them. They included a divorced doctor, a woman who had survived cancer, a woman who had traveled the world, someone who lost their relatives, a young guy who had a bit of an addiction problem, a psychologist... and then there was shaman Tom and his bromance-friend Dan, from the South Dakota trip.

"We all have some problems that we keep inside. This place will take it all out of you. This place will. With your heart, and ayahuasca." I listened to the voice behind me. Someone was talking. I looked at the mountains in the distant landscape and started to be a bit shaky. There he was. He just appeared like a ghost. He was standing in front of me probably, under five feet (150 cm) tall—a real Peruvian Inca with only a few teeth left in his mouth. With that huge toothless smile, he said, "Hi, are you with us?"

What does he mean, with us? I thought.

Green—his light was green. It was so bright, and shining from his heart. I felt warm, so warm and safe. This little unconditional love was standing in front of me. His face was looking at me, with tiny brown eyes. I couldn't tell his age. *Forty? Fifty? Sixty? No clue.* He had a very bright hat and little bag on his side full of coca leaves. He was the Peruvian shaman-friend of my shaman, Tom. *Another shaman on my list*, I thought. *Well compared to huge Ed in South Dakota, this one is quite tiny—but their strength is measured by the power of their hearts, not by their body size.*

"Yes, coming!" I jumped into our bus, with the warm feeling that everything would be how it should, because this little shaman had a heart of gold which was bigger than him and this bus together. *Inca's heart.*

Tower of Light

"Here, hold this coca leaf while we drive and pray. The energy is strong here." He winked at me, as if he knew I was getting dizzy. Well, he probably did. His wisdom was huge, and he was thankful and humble. He was the shaman of the ayahuasca plant, and he knew how to protect human energy and how to speak to spirits. He was doing it with all love and care.

His nickname was Cucho, but he started using his birth name, Juan Díaz, in 2012. That was when he knew the energy changed, when he knew to give information to others—not only to Incas or Peruvians, but also to the "gringos" like us. I didn't know yet that I would change my name a year later, too. He was listening to the spirits of the whole world here, and on other levels, which these people were about to experience. He knew that the world was changing. We came here to listen and learn with respect for this Earth, called Mamacocha, so that we would be able to share further with our world. These people knew you have to start somewhere to share the wisdom. You cannot change anything until you can understand and change yourself.

"Yesterday I wanted to change the world, but today I am changing myself," I whispered into Lukas the filmmaker's ear in the bus to Cusco. He was quiet. I knew that this journey wouldn't be something to chat about in a bar after. The respect and silence about all of it has to be placed here, right here in each of our hearts, and kept there. I looked at his camera and was wondering if the camera could capture what we were about to experience. I closed my eyes and imagined the light from my accident. *Well no one could take a pic of that, but we all somehow hope it exists.* I felt it exists in each of us. I felt it even more when we got to the Peruvian city of Cusco.

"All of you, close your eyes. Don't open them, no matter what. Hold each other's hands, make a row, and walk with closed eyes. Don't break the magic." Juan Díaz, our shaman, the tiny Inca man, was standing half a mile under the top of Machu Picchu—and had a plan for us. "Don't open your eyes no matter what." We couldn't see the top. We had no idea how close we were. We were on a rocky road, surrounded by trees.

The thirteen of us started walking in a row. I was holding hands with Mary Carol and Reena toward the front of this snake-like line of adults. It was like being in kindergarten, except that we were all adults, walking blind. It was hard to walk with closed eyes in a row of thirteen people. We were all very quiet. *Left, right, left, right...* I could feel the rocks underneath my boots.

"You need to put your feet to the ground and feel it with every step. It is like a life. Feel the ground with every step. Be thankful that you can walk; be thankful to be on the ground; and make your way to the top. Trust yourself. No fear," he whispered into the breeze, which started to be stronger.

"Stop. Turn around and keep your eyes closed," Juan said. Reena's hand got sweaty, Mary's hand got cold. I felt my heart in my hand vibrating. When someone took my backpack, I panicked; but I let them take the heavy part away from me. *If it's a thief, oh well; the heavy load from my back is gone. Just GONE.* I didn't open my eyes. I didn't want to break the magic for all of them. I could feel the breeze blowing in front of me, into my face.

Tower of Light

"NOW OPEN," he said. We did—and with that my heart blasted. There it was. We were two feet from a steep cliff at the edge of the mountain, and in front of us was Machu Picchu. All I could feel was POWER. That moment brought tears to my eyes. We all were still holding hands and shaking. We all felt the power of that old mountain. We all were quiet and touched. It was the mountain from my dream, I saw that clearly now. I had been here before in my dreams, and in my past life, too. It was stronger than déjà-vu; I felt like I was home. I knew every piece of that mountain. I knew it so well that I was just standing there and stared at it. I felt Love; it was green like the color of the heart chakra light energy I see sometimes in humans.

This is the center of Love. Maybe not everyone's, but mine for sure. We all have places that somehow have been calling us. They are calling us because we were there, many times before. We go back to those places to understand *why. I am finally here. I am alive, and I am here.*

I realized how close we were from the cliff, and I stepped back and looked around. They all were smiling. All of the people in our group were smiling and in tears at the same time, including shaman Tom. I smiled back at him and thanked him with that smile. *I met him so that he would bring me here. I met him in his Chicago office exactly one year ago to find out who I am, and to come here.* He knew. I saw the vision of him holding my body, my man body, when I died, and carrying me into those stairs. He always loved me, he always helped me, and he prayed for me when I died here. He was always around for my rebirths too, and I had many—I was an old soul. Here I was in the body of a blonde little girl, but feeling the warrior in me.

I haven't needed to chew on coca leaves since then. That mountain gave me air to breathe, and the ground to stand. I was from that mountain, and I was born there, too. I felt very strong and masculine energy going through my body. I knew I was a warrior here. I wished for everyone to see who they truly are—not to pretend, just to be. If fragile, if mean, if sad, if happy, if gay, if trans, if a woman, if a man, if depressed, if lost… just to know who they really are and accept it. YOUR OWN ACCEPTANCE IS BEAUTIFUL.

"There, there was a fire with bodies on it," I pointed to a bit of stone that I could see far off down the mountain.

"It is just a stone. Or you mean a barbecue in Peru?" Lukas said as he continued filming the surroundings.

"No, silly—there was a fire, I know it." I started pointing down far away in the horizon. Juan, our shaman, came closer to me and smiled.

"Yes, princess warrior, there was a fire. In old times it was a funeral place of fire, for people to pray when they died. I know you know. You are working with fire now. I would like to work with you. You will build something beautiful." I wasn't surprised when he called me "princess warrior." I wasn't surprised that he knew I paint with fire. *I know I am. He knows I am.*

"I need a Peruvian hairband, to cover my third eye," I told him as I touched my forehead.

"Why? Don't you want to know more? I want to see more," he said in surprise.

Tower of Light

"I don't. This is enough. You are living in Peru, but I can't go for a week to sleep in a cave and say 'adios.' I live in a big city in the USA." I started laughing and holding his hand, and I felt so happy to open up and finally say what I see.

"...and there, there was a sun praying tower, people were wishing good things there." I couldn't catch my breath and was pointing at the place underneath Machu Picchu. I saw the whole thing. It wasn't from a night vision or my dream. It wasn't a hallucination. I was standing there during broad daylight, and it was a strong feeling of information. I saw the whole crystal city during the time of the Incas. I knew that place... I saw a spaceship above it. That was a weird one... *Aliens? Hmmmmm, not sure.*

I automatically put my vibrating hands to the sky, closed my eyes, and said, "Heal me, heal me and all of the souls in this world," and I truly meant it. It was so natural. I knew I was standing there many, many, many lifetimes before and doing the same thing. I felt home, and closer to the light. I felt this place and saw how many beautiful souls were praying and wishing better things for the world here. I felt the whole civilization and information which had been forgotten.

We forgot. We knew all of it, way before. We knew how powerful we were, how connected we could be to the light. How thankful we should be. We knew the strength of the Earth and Light. We knew all about the love and light and connections and life cycle. We just somehow forgot... We just got too "busy" and stopped listening. I didn't feel sad about this truth. I didn't judge anyone, myself or others. I wasn't upset about what we did or didn't do in this world. I took it as a call, a call I could hear through my heart. A call from nature, a call from the Earth, and a call from all of history. I felt recharged.

I felt HOPE—and right there I felt that I would never ever give up that HOPE. No matter what people from the USA would think, no matter what people from Europe or Asia or the whole planet would think, no matter who I would talk to, and I saw how many I would need to talk to. And I saw the resistance. *I will talk to many people from different levels of society...* I felt it strongly inside me, but with no fear.

Right there, I felt the reason why I was sent back. I saw the towers that used to be on the top of this mountain, and I felt hope for humanity in my heart. I felt the energy of the whole universe. I felt the change; not only in me, but in people. That change is coming. I realized later that right there, I saw the TOWER OF LIGHT for a split second.

"If you came here to learn something about this place, you could get a regular guide, or google it. I am not here to teach you anything you can read on the internet." This is what our Peruvian shaman said as we were again standing in a thirteen-person line beneath Machu Picchu. He was standing in front of us in white a t-shirt, still smiling. He was always smiling, and I knew it was not because of the amount of coca leaves he was chewing. He was just at peace with this place.

"Can you imagine Juan, this Inca shaman, talking like that on Facetime?" I smiled at Reena.

"Maybe he can Skype too, man," she said, and made a funny face.

"Dude, this guy can skype with no computer, phone, or iPad," I winked at her.

After our hiking experience, we smoked organic tobacco and made a wish. We sang and OHM-ed together in many places, and we were quiet when he spoke about the traditions of those times. Our group of thirteen travelers was different from the other groups of Machu Picchu tourists. We knew it. Everyone who saw this little guy guiding us on the trails respectfully bowed their head to him. All of them knew him, and if they didn't, they could recognize the shaman spirit in him. This shaman was a very respected soul in Machu Picchu.

His assistant, Ira, was about 6'4" (2 meters) tall, and together those two made a funny-looking pair. Sometimes they played music on whistles while we were walking and he was talking about their wisdom. It was the most beautiful time, but I was always aware that the night of ayahuasca was getting closer, and I was nervous. The scar on my head started to be itchy, and I knew why.

Coca Leaf Reading

"Tu estas aquí..."

"You are here..." one member of our group was translating the words spoken by Ira, the tall assistant to our small medicine man. When he pointed his finger at me, I didn't feel comfortable—I felt the way I did the night before my accident. I knew I needed to leave my comfort zone in order to grow. I didn't resist the feeling, I only observed.

Misa Art

I was sitting inside a tiny house in front of the house of the ayahuasca ceremony. We had one hour to go inside and drink this spirit of wisdom. It started to be a dark night. I didn't feel right. Ira was reading from my coca leaves. He spread them in front of me like the cards of a tarot reader. He was staring at the leaves, which all seemed about the same and to me—green. He was reading them like there was a story written in those veins of nature. He continued in Spanish.

"You are here, and the mountain is talking to you. But you refuse to listen fully. You are strong, a very strong spirit. You are like a warrior. You should work with shamanic women. Your gift comes from your grandmother and her mother. They were, too."

As soon as he said it, a very tall silhouette appeared behind him. I saw him again for a split second—*my guardian*. He moved his head left and right, then he was gone.

"You work with children, you work with them and you paint. They are here to teach us..." He was chewing on coca leaves and continued staring at them.

If a child doesn't know how to learn, maybe we should change the way of teaching that child. That was what I thought at that moment. He continued in Spanish, and it felt a bit like he was yelling at me. He was serious and intense.

"You had... you had an experience... hm... You saw, and you have a gift to see." He looked at me. "What do you want to ask me?" He felt my protector as well. He didn't want to talk to me. I could feel it. He could see my third eye.

Tower of Light

"I am asking you if I can do ayahuasca, if I can drink the medicine," I asked quietly. He paused. The door opened, and our tiny shaman Juan was inside. He only walked inside to grab something before the ceremony. Everyone was getting ready.

Ira was quiet.

"I know I shouldn't," I continued, and didn't pay attention to his nervous face.

"I shouldn't be telling you... my master is here. But if you do, drink very little. You are already there, you saw," he replied while he put his head down and collected all the leaves together. He was done with my coca leaf reading. My translating friend next to him was staring at me with an open mouth.

"I know it is not my time to do so. I know I wouldn't return. I would stay there. I wouldn't return back here to this Earth. I am already a bit in-between," I said in Spanish and got up. I looked up and felt my guardian again. At that moment I felt love for that tall Ira. Somehow I saw his path and pain; two years later we found out that this coca leaf reader died at the age of thirty-three. I did see his spirit go at that tiny house close to Machu Picchu—maybe that's why he didn't feel comfortable talking to me.

Little Juan turned around and jumped into our conversation.

"It is ok, princess warrior, you had an accident a year ago… it is too early for you, you have already seen. You can stay during the ceremony, but you have to be quiet and only observe." There was no shaman in this world who would let you stay during an ayahuasca ceremony and not take the magic medicine. He could see my gift, my gift to see. He knew I saw a lot during, before, and after my accident. I was happy to have the switch. I was not looking for more information that I couldn't handle. I knew my limits and I saw my guardian. I remembered those times when I couldn't handle it and it gave me chills. I was still like a one-year-old baby with lots of new information.

"Thank you." I smiled at him. I was a bit disappointed, because I knew that I had experienced many levels of consciousness during my accident. But I also knew we shouldn't be overdoing things or pushing ourselves, no matter how much we would like to. It will all come naturally. I knew that my experience was there for me to keep, and that I needed to listen to no one but me and my inner-self—no shamans, no readers, no humans. *I am here to follow no one, only to feel the light.*

I grabbed my blanket and walked inside a tall, huge room. There were ten people from our group including my urban-shaman-friend, Tom. They all had buckets and blankets and were sitting on pillows. They all had questions in their hearts. *But are you all ready to see the truth? …or not?* The truth can be very raw. I felt very cold.

I sat next to my friends Reena and Mary, in order to feel more grounded. Whenever you feel fear of the unknown, it is good to sit next to something or someone familiar. I knew this was not a "group thing," that at the end we are alone in this journey. It is you and you only. I knew I would feel them all.

The scar in the back of my head started to be itchy again, and my forehead felt warm. I remembered a childhood swimming lesson: "To be floating in the water you have to relax and have faith. If you start to grab the water in panic, you will drown." *Same in life, and same as with this plant and this ceremony.* With no fear, only an open heart, I was proud of them.

Ayahuasca Medicina

Whuzzzzzzzzzuuuuuu... I was sitting on a big pillow during the ceremony. We were all around a huge circle in the house close to Machu Picchu. I could hear the river far away. It was a calm, beautiful night.

Whuzzzzzzzzzzuuuuuu... the sound vibrated through my body.

Our little shaman was pushing air into a big shell making a beautiful sound. The sound traveled in the middle of our circle. *Whuzzz...* it sounded like the same sound I heard when I was on that street, when I didn't feel my body. Chills went up my spine. I closed my eyes. *So this is the sound of my soul... the shell! I heard this sound before, when I was leaving my body.* Once someone told me, "It is in the Bible, the sounds of trumpets when you are close to heaven..."

The shaman started to sing a beautiful song in Spanish. I saw a vision of people in churches. I saw Amma too. People in this room took a little shot of ayahuasca. I didn't. They all puked into the bucket next to them. *Detox of the physical... the spirits are coming.*

I felt cold, very cold... I felt the powerful presence of this healing spirit called ayahuasca.

A huge green snake started to appear behind shaman's back, with the rhythm of his music the neon snake went around and entered them, one by one. The spirit of ayahuasca stopped in front of me. I closed my eyes and said, "I didn't take you, but I respect you." It paused, then passed me.

Ira's face changed. He was sitting next to our shaman. A big panther came in front of him. The divorce doctor's face turned neon. I saw very tall alien spirits coming into the circle. I saw many personal things entering them, one by one. I saw medicine spirits with a serious face talking to Reena. I saw a big huge tarantula in front of one of them. It was like a movie. I felt the shaman's heart, how he cared for all of their trouble, love, and pain. He was like a conductor, protecting them with music and shooting unconditional love through his heart around the circle. He was glowing with love and care. This ceremony was going on in waves for five hours. I was quiet and felt just love. I was sitting in the middle of it. When I closed my eyes I saw Machu Picchu and was flying through those mountain alleys of it. I could hear the rain. It was really, really dark by the end, because the lights around all of them had died down.

People who know this medicine have the saying: "Whatever you ask ayahuasca, she will show you." Through this medicine some people have healed their addiction, their sorrow—if you really listen, she will show you all, the light, too, all in a raw form. If you are ready, she will show you all. If you are not, she will show you nothing, and you will only puke all night.

"I am so sorry you have to know so much," Reena said as she crawled closer to me, and I held her in my arms after the ceremony. They all cried, during or after, and they all had a bit of a different look about them. They were all quiet.

"You have neon eyes and grey hair, you are so old!" she whispered, and I knew in that moment she saw the wisdom I had received on that street a year ago. For that split second of her ayahuasca experience, she saw my light... I knew she was my little soul sister.

"It's ok. I am ok, I know what to do with it, don't you worry! Don't worry about other people. Give yourself love first," I said, and hugged her.

Ira passed by us as I was hugging her.

"You are a panther," I said. He stopped and stared at me.

"That's what the American Indians call me, how do you know?" I just smiled.

Later, I painted all of their experiences.

Amazonia

"Smooth sea never made a skilled sailor." We were going to the Monkey Forest in Amazonia on a small boat to meet the next Peruvian shaman.

Misa Art

There's my Chicago shaman, Juan Díaz from Machu Picchu, and now we are supposed to meet "shaman number three" in the middle of Amazonia. He was a Christian. So he is doing the ayahuasca ceremony with all those saints and bringing them to the ceremony... I got a weird feeling from him and couldn't see the pure light. It was only my feeling, and I listened.

When I saw him, I knew that he was not a type of soul that I would let my spirit into his hands. I just didn't feel it. I didn't do an ayahuasca ceremony with him either, and he didn't let me stay. So when everyone left to do a second round, I stayed in one of the houses in Amazonia alone. In the middle of the night, I woke up and saw a bright star in my room. I was shaking—it was similar to a light I had seen before. It was strong, like Jesus's light on the street of my hit-and-run.

My friends came, and were shaking too. It was very strong energy. He was too strong of a spirit leader for me. It is important to choose your spiritual leaders wisely, just as when you choose your friends wisely, or when you choose books and other information from the media, TV, and radio. Only you can choose, and don't judge those who are not for you, just let them go. I collect leaders of Love—not those with the love of power, but only those who are the power of love and give love unconditionally.

When I returned from Peru, I took the peace of that land with me in my heart. It is so beautiful to do so. Whenever you have traveled to a place you like, you can just close your eyes and imagine the peace you felt in that place. In that way, you can carry many places in your heart. It always reminded me of when I was homesick and missed my home—I always did that. For a while after the journey, if I had to face business problems at the children's foundation or had to deal with art shows or other personal or financial problems, I used to say, "Don't mess with my peace from Peru!" Then I laughed, because it always helped— maybe not with the problems, but with the way I looked at them. If you cannot change things, just change the way you look at them.

I remembered that little shaman, Juan—how thankful he was, and how I cried when we had to say goodbye at the airport to him. I knew I would see him one day; I knew that day would come. When he was drinking water, Juan always gave a couple of drops to the Earth before every sip. I did it in the airport as well.

"Not on the cement, silly princess warrior!" I made him laugh after I spilled a little water in the middle of Cusco airport. It was my "blonde" moment.

"You have to give it to the Earth… *there*," and he pointed outside of the airport. "…and be thankful," he said as I was laughing at my silly mistake. "That's right, but I tried, trying counts, too." I winked at him and said goodbye to his beautiful, giving heart, and with that, to that amazing place. I walked outside and spilled a few drops of water on the ground of Peru before my flight back. I felt blessed and thankful. I started to understand why I had come here.

"The file is not there—I mean, the file is there, but no one can open it—it's all gone. The whole film is gone. I sent it to Germany, and no one can open it." My filmmaker friend was on the phone a couple of days later after we returned from Peru. He was talking fast and was very upset. I smiled at the phone speaker.

"The spirits of Machu Picchu just didn't want anyone to see. Magic." He knew that it was the truth, and that the journey could be kept only in our hearts, not on the film. Sometimes we should just accept the way things are and believe that there is a reason for everything.

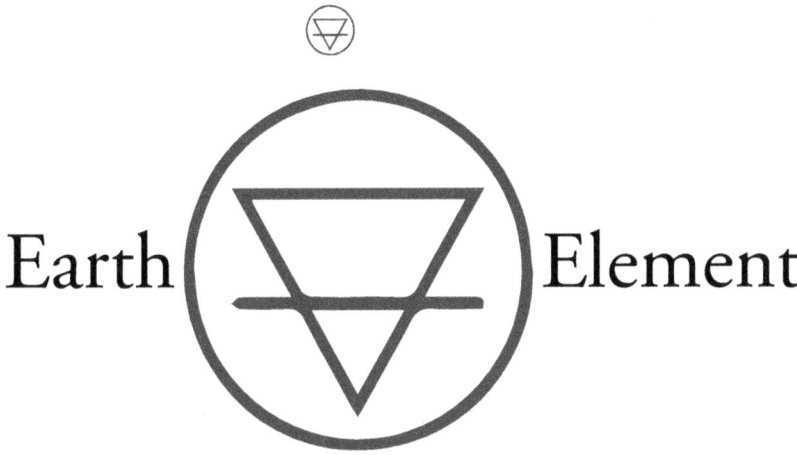

"Never stop dreaming, and if possible, try to make them come true, but always remember your limits."

"There is only one thing to do, and that is to take the journey into our soul."

Chapter 13

Tower of Light

Tower of Light

"What do you have on your forehead?"

My mom was looking at me from the Skype screen.

"I don't know... but it looks like a mark or something."

"That's crazy" I had this strange sign in the middle of my forehead for a couple of days, and then it disappeared.

"It looked like a little tower," I smiled, "right in the place of my third eye..."

"Stigmata Misa," my shaman playfully texted me after I sent him a picture of my forehead. But I could feel that information was entering my head—heavily.

I was back in busy Chicago. After a couple of days, I started to have dreams—dreams about the Towers of Light, architectural structures that would bring hope, and help people believe in light and love. The dreams were so vivid.

I wanted people to believe in something good. I could feel the whole world suffering. I could feel all of people's stories, diseases, and love stories. I didn't want to make them believe in any kind of religion, just to feel the love and give themselves up to the power of their wishes; not any wishes, but *wishes*—the intentions that come from our souls and our purpose here on Earth.

I wanted to share all that I was feeling. I started to write every day about this tower structure. The TOWER OF LIGHT would be for them, for everyone to understand the energy levels in our body, to understand the connection to this Earth. It would be a structure that would help artists around the world. I knew there were no awards for visual art—to be a visual artist you need to have a gift, and the purpose of this gift is to share and give it away. This tower would bring awards for visual artists, too. This TOWER OF LIGHT would help nonprofit organizations for children.

Some people have the fear that they won't make it, that in this world you must be "perfect" and " successful." But I knew now that nothing and no one is perfect. That is what is beautiful. That is ART. So I transformed all of that wisdom into this structure.

We all have a gift, and the gift is that light. This tower would be made to help people so that when they touch it, they will feel the light in that moment. It will help artists and all children's foundations raise money for kids in need. The dreams were coming in detail. Every day I woke up and was writing details—astrological, technical, and business structure as well. As soon as I wrote it, I forgot what I had written—it was coming through me and out. I was living and breathing for this project, because I knew that I was not doing it in order to become some famous artist. I knew that this was the reason I was sent back to this Earth. This was the reason my whole existence changed, and I wanted everyone to feel the light. This was the reason I had my awakening, the reason I transformed from a party girl into this messenger of love.

Tower of Light

The sign in the middle of my forehead went away, but I knew I needed to calm down on thinking about this Tower of Light. It was lots of information to handle. I'm not saying that I felt like knowing all this information somehow put me above people, or that my purpose is bigger than anyone else's. The purpose for everyone is the same: to heal, to change patterns, to do good things, and to learn how to give and receive love. It is simple. I felt humble. I saw the resistance that would come from some people, and maybe envy, but I still didn't stop. I had hope and that light in my heart. How in the world did I suddenly understand astrological, psychological, and spiritual things? I don't know. It was my heart connecting to the source. I knew that this TOWER OF LIGHT would be able to convey the message further. It is for people, not for me; it comes from that light, which is so difficult to explain in words. It is all in that tower... all life, all being. I started to do this for you and you and you—and for everyone that exists.

I just needed an architect first, my inner voice said.

I was sitting in my studio every day—while I worked, while I was on the phone, while I painted paintings to hold me over financially—and I worked nonstop.

I prayed: "Please bring me someone who can do this with me." I was manifesting every day, closing my eyes, and wishing for that. I was not only sitting, I was searching everywhere. It was on my mind all the time. It was something that didn't let me sleep, and I knew—I just knew that I had to do this. I was patient, because I could feel it coming. My King Kath was always supporting me in times when I doubted myself. Those times came sometimes, but I had Kath and other people who trusted my love and intuition. When I finally learned how to ask, they gave me support and kept pushing me. Those who didn't, I just didn't talk to. I didn't need their fear, or to hear from them that my goals were "impossible."

I knew from that light and my life experiences that the word "impossible" just doesn't exist. Someone even told me, "This will kill you." I smiled and said, "Great, I already died once, I am ok with it, hahaha!" I moved on from those negative vibes and started knocking on different doors. When you have something you know in your heart is good, listen only to yourself. There will always be those who doubt you; just smile at them and wish them well. I knew it would be a long journey. I was blessed to have my life back, and I wanted to give this love to help everyone feel it.

"Hi, I am an architect for your friend and I just wanted to check out your studio," said a middle-aged bald man who walked into my studio two weeks later. I scanned him with my eyes. *Beautiful mind, beautiful heart, and well-integrated ego. Perfect for my project.*

"Hi, good! Here is my art, and I need to talk to you about this project. I knew I would meet you, and we would build the Tower of Hope together. I want to build many everywhere, all over in the world." I blasted it straight at him.

He was confused, as he had just met me—but I knew. I asked for him, and he came. It really works. Just ask. I am asking you, all of you, to ask for things, and if they are supposed to be on your path, they will come. It is simple. Ask directly and clearly, and they will come. It is the law of the universe. It is the law of Love and of Light.

I started to work with Douglas on the TOWER OF LIGHT. We planned it all out, and within eleven months we had become great friends. Later that year, I met another architect named Zenon to help out and give his opinion on the structure. During that time I was "scanning" people everywhere I went. My gift of intuition and reading was the best thing for me now. The same gift I didn't want to have before became my best guiding source. I started to use it for good.

Tower of Light

I scanned people in the middle of crowds—artists, politicians, creative, not creative... I walked directly up to people, pointed at them and said: "YOU! I need to talk to you." I scanned them by the light, and I started to create a group of people to help build this structure. They were people with different beliefs and from different levels of society, but all with a similar light. They all had that kind light of hope.

It wasn't an ordinary structure. I knew I was bringing something pure down to Earth, and I knew that the wishes people made in the TOWER OF LIGHT needed to go further in order to really happen and come true. The wishes needed to help many people, not just one person. It wasn't a structure or any kind of art piece to show my skills or for people to admire. It was an interactive piece of love for everyone to experience. Even if it didn't work in the same way that some people expected, if even for a second it brought peace and light to those people, it would be a good thing. It will take some time to build it, but once it is finished people will feel it—the energy of those towers and my message. It wouldn't be something to think about, but only to feel. It was an ART of LOVE and a PLACE of ZEN.

To have dreams is a beautiful thing, but when you don't take the steps to realize them, they are only hallucinations. DON'T STOP. DO IT. Follow your dreams. Be patient, and LISTEN.

I spoke like this to myself every day. I was born stubborn, that I knew. But I also knew that I could change my stubbornness into patience.

I knew this would be a long journey of investors, organizations, and resistance—maybe greed for money, or people's need to be seen in public or to be famous—but I knew the roots of it were Pure. It is Pure Light and Love. And I knew my own ego was leveled. Some people say to me, "This is some artist's joke and fantasy of yours." Oh well, good for them. Everyone is doing the best they can from their own current level of consciousness and awareness.

Misa Art

I knew I wouldn't get upset at the fact that some people wouldn't help or understand. I was used to not being understood. I didn't have the need to be understood. I knew I would only wish them well, because one day we all will see the light and hope. One day we all will, when we leave this world. So why not take life and make it beautiful and colorful, and radiantly pure through the LOVE of ART? The next generation will understand this more, I know, and after them more, and more. This structure, which came to me through the vision of the Tower of Light, was from the ancient past, but somehow it was 60 – 100 years ahead of its time. I knew this world was ready for the Tower of Light. I knew this world needed it. I felt it so strongly. It was deep inside me, and the light reminded me and pushed me forward every day. I had meetings and met hundreds of people in Chicago, New York City, Los Angeles, Miami, and Europe. I am continuing to manifest the vision to build the monument of Goodness.

We as humans were building monuments to celebrate the past or grief—monuments of people who died, or monuments to remind us of wars and loss.

These towers, TOWER OF LIGHT will celebrate the present and presence of our own being.

This structure will celebrate Goodness with no judgment, no restrictions, and no rules.

People will make their wish each time they visit. Every day it will feel different for you.

Every two years this project will move to a different city in the USA so that the Tower of Light will come to everyone. Every two years, the Tower of Light will move to different cities in Europe as well to remind people of their light and hope there, too.

Tower of Light

If you are reading this book, please look around and look inside yourself and have the belief that good things will happen, and that hope exists, and please wish for the Tower of Light wherever you are, because it will be built with Love to shine back upon you and many others with love. I was sent here to do so, I will not give up hope for my vision.

Hope is the vision itself, the Towers of hope, TOWER OF LIGHT. One day, I would like to warmly invite you to come and touch the tower yourself and to make a wish and to stand tall in that wish, like a tower of light, shining brightly for all those who may be without hope, to feel the light, and to see the light. That is why I am here, to shine as the light of LOVE... just like YOU.

It is exactly eight years ago that I heard that sentence from my Shaman friend, when I was lost and without that Light of Hope. I remember standing, lost in his office. After the "ghost party on my body," when he was talking about my "ghosts," he told me:

"When you are a light you bring them to you, but one day you turn them into light and they will help you. Because love is ALWAYS there."

I didn't understand that at the time, and stood there with the question, "So I'm going to help turn a thousand 'ghosts' towards the light?"

I smile now, because the Tower of Light *is* that light. We should understand and accept the dark parts of ourselves in order to come closer and to truly appreciate and understand the light and love, because the LOVE is always there, no matter how many "ghosts" we have or how many different roads or decisions we make. We are all born to be the light.

Love,

Misa

Tower  of light

"Tower of Light joins the human state (grounding) with our finding of inner strength(love), earthly capabilities(energy), and powerful aspirations(hope-light)"

"Upon the moment of each hour's arrival light-seekers will have an opportunity to make their wish, informed upon each tower of what its chakra (energy or element) 're-present'"

Each chapter (chakras, elements) of this book matches each tower in this sculptural interactive project - Tower of Light.

Congratulations on your new experience. :)

Copyright © of Tower of Light Misa Art. Architectural design with-by Douglas Hammen. All right reserved for book Tower of Light neither for sculptural project Tower of Light No part of publication may be reproduced, distributed or transmitted in any form or by any means, including photocopying, recording, or other mechanical methods, without the prior written permission of the innovator Misa ART.

Epilogue

Never-Ending Circle of Light

I was standing by his bed. He was lying there, dying. His face was old and in pain. I could feel how I had always been meeting him—now, then, and before.

"Forgive me," he whispered.

"I forgive you," I answered, and I hugged him. His face was similar to mine—I had forgotten that, as it had been so long since I saw him last. It was a long time ago when I called this man "my dad." I felt I forgave him for me. I felt if I didn't, he might come back in my next life as my child, my blood.

I slowly left the room and started to walk from that dark building to the street. From the space between the open main door, I could see the huge beam of light shining to the sky. There they were - the shining steel towers. It was the Tower of Light, shining in the middle of the city square into people. They were all standing there, receiving light and making wishes.

Tower of Light

I woke up. I sat up on the bed and slowly opened my eyes. But this time I wasn't sweating, I was calm. I just smiled and laid back down on the bed and hugged the warm eagle-man next to me.

"Are you ok, baby? Bad dream again?" He whispered from his sleep and hugged me. I felt like I was free-falling from his caring touch.

"I am ok, love. And everything will be—maybe not in time, but with time." I answered with peace in my heart.

About the Author

Misa Art

Tower of Light

About the Author

I believe in miracles.

International artist Misa is originally from the Czech Republic, and she has also lived in Chicago, New York City, Florida and now, California. Her artistic emphasis has been the study of color and its emotional impact on our well-being. Whether on wood or metal, the rhythm of Misa's brushstrokes, a flowing mix of muted color with the contrapuntal pull of feelings and inspiration, transforms realismus into an equally intense observation of surface. Her signature style blends several artistic genres into a blissful harmony. It needs no interpretation. Her work crosses all borders and boundaries to create an expression of spirit and beauty that all audiences can relate to.

"THROUGH MY WORK, I aspire to bring our visions, feelings, thoughts and inspiration to LIFE"

MY ART: misa-artwork.com
Facebook: facebook.com/misa.art
Instagram: instagram.com/misaart/
ART Gallery: facebook.com/MisaandMartin/
Twitter: twitter/misaart

PAST NONPROFIT ORGANIZATION FOR CHILDREN:
misaforlove.org

Contents

1. Chapter (Root, Red, First Chakra)
   "GHOST PARTY ON MY BODY"
   Painting: Love Hangover, 2010
   Media: acrylic, wood, fire
   34"x 48"

2. Chapter (Spleen Center, Orange, Second Chakra)
   "DREAMS OF PREDICTIONs"
   Painting: ZULU-Goddess of Prediction, 2009,
   Media : wood, acrylics, fire
   48"x 39"

3. Chapter (Solar-Plexus, Yellow, Third Chakra)
   "SWEAT and FEAR
   Painting: Golden Mandala, 2016
   Media: acrylics, wood fire, grinders
   62"x 42" 4 panels.

4. Chapter (Anahata-Heart, Green, Fourth Chakra)
   "FLYING GEISHA"
   Painting: Protection, 2012
   Media: canvas, acrylics
   48'x 50"

5. Chapter (Throat, Blue, Fifth Chakra)
   "ANGELS AND PRAYERS"
   Painting: Dance with Light 2013
   Media: copper, acrylics, fire, patina
   48"x 32"

6. Chapter (Third-eye, Indigo Sixth Chakra)
   "THE POWER OF MANIFESTATION"
   Painting: Calm Waters, 2018.
   Media: copper, acrylics, patina.
   48" x36"

7. Chapter (Crown Chakra, Violet, Seventh Chakra)
"NATIVE AMERICAN INDIANS"
Painting: FEATHER 2017
Media: copper, patina, grinder
42"x 28"

8. Chapter (Element UNIVERSE)
"KING AND PRIEST"
Painting: RELIGIOSA< Buddha awakening.
Media: copper, patina, acrylics
48"x 36"

9. Chapter (Element WATER)
"AMMA"
Painting: Farah of Grace 2008
Media: wood, fire, acrylics
53'x 42"

10, Chapter (Element AIR)
"TAROT READER, EAGLES AND PIGEONS"
Painting: Feather, 2018
Media: stainless steel, acrylics
14'x14'

11. Chapter (Element FIRE)
"SOULMATES AND TWIN FLAMES"
Painting: Dandelions 2019
Media: stainless steel, acrylics, fire
20"x12"

12. Chapter (Element EARTH)
"MAMACOCHA"
Painting: Angel View 2017,
Media: copper, fire, acrylics,
48'x 32"

13. Chapter (Tower of Light)
"TOWERS OF LIGHT"
Design by Misa Art, Douglas Hammen.
ALL COPYRIGHTS © TO MISA ART
AND DOUGLAS HAMMEN